D1234368

THE ROAD TO TYBURN

ع

Jack Sheppard

from the painting by Sir James Thornhill, engraved by
George White

THE ROAD TO TYBURN

THE STORY OF JACK SHEPPARD AND
THE EIGHTEENTH-CENTURY LONDON UNDERWORLD

BY

CHRISTOPHER HIBBERT

THE WORLD PUBLISHING COMPANY

CLEVELAND AND NEW YORK

Published by THE WORLD PUBLISHING COMPANY

2231 West 110th Street, Cleveland 2, Ohio

Library of Congress Catalog Card Number: 57–10935

FIRST EDITION

For Sue

NOTE

——

THIS biography of Jack Sheppard is based mainly on contemporary pamphlets, newspapers, and trial reports in the British Museum, the Bodleian Library, and the Inner Temple Library. It is intended as a work of entertainment rather than of scholarship; but for those who may be interested I have added a list of books of which I have made use in filling in the background to Sheppard's strange story. Of recent writers I am particularly indebted to Dr. M. Dorothy George, Mr. Peter Quennell, Mr. Patrick Pringle, and Dr. Leon Radzinowicz.

I am also indebted to the late Horace Bleackley for some details of Sheppard's early life and family taken from parish records and given in his brief account of Sheppard's life in the Notable British Trials series.

The details of Sheppard's extraordinary adventures are obscure and the authorities are sometimes contradictory and often intentionally sensational. In sorting and checking these authorities I am very grateful for the

7

assistance given to me by Miss Mary Cosh, whose experience and discernment have been most helpful.

Various slang words and phrases, which are now no longer in use, will be found in the reported conversations of criminals and in the depositions of witnesses at their trials. I have not explained these in the text, but I have included a glossary of eighteenth-century criminal cant as an appendix. This glossary is not exhaustive, but all the cant words quoted in the book, and most others in common use at the time, are translated there.

CONTENTS

———

Contents

ILLUSTRATIONS

———

*The frontispiece and the illustrations facing pages 113 and 192 are
reproduced from engravings in the Department of
Prints and Drawings, British Museum.*

THE ROAD TO TYBURN

CHAPTER ONE

THE LEGEND

—

THE prison gate opened and he came out into the
cobbled street smiling to the crowd. It was a cold
damp November morning, but he had no hat and
he wore his coat more for effect than for warmth. His
hands were clasped in front of him and the full fashionable
cuffs of the smart black coat concealed the thick handcuffs
round his wrists.

He was a curiously impressive little figure. Very slim
and scarcely more than five feet four inches in height, it
was difficult to believe the stories of his amazing strength
and endurance that had made him the most famous criminal of his time. There was nothing in the features of his
intelligent face just as there was nothing in his behaviour
to suggest the "dirty blackguard" of Francis Place or
the "brutal scoundrel" described by Thackeray. His
short black hair and thick black eyebrows emphasized the
pallor of his skin while his upturned nose and immense

brown eyes gave the impression of a personality at once arresting and pathetic. Although he was now twenty-two years old he looked little more than eighteen and many of those who saw him now for the first time were surprised not so much by his proud unconcern as by his look of youthful innocence.

He stepped up into the open cart and saw without apparent shock the forbidding figure of the common hangman sitting on his coffin. He sat down behind the hangman next to Wagstaff, the Newgate chaplain, and listened more out of politeness than conviction to the prayers and admonitions which Parson Wagstaff whispered in his ear, nodding sometimes, making an occasional comment, but all the time holding his head high and looking around him. Throughout the long ride to Tyburn gallows he kept up this careful watchfulness, his sharp eyes scanning the faces in the crowd, looking for a signal, a warning, an encouragement. He never, it seems, for a moment supposed that he would not escape. Certainly many of the tens of thousands of people who lined the route to Tyburn and crowded round the enormous triple gallows, to get a good view of "the hanging match," expected him to do so and hoped that he would do so.

For three months now he had been the most talked of man in London. During his recent imprisonment in the Condemned Hold at Newgate he had been visited by hundreds of curious people who had paid a generous fee to his jailers to see him or to talk to him, to amuse them-

selves by listening to the stories of his escapades told
with a bright Cockney wit in a voice made attractive by
a slight stammer. He had been painted, it was said at the
suggestion of King George himself, by Sir James Thornhill, the Serjeant Painter to the crown and since the death
of Kneller the most fashionable artist of his day. He had
given an account of his life and adventures to Daniel
Defoe, whose subsequent version of his history was one
of at least ten published within a few months of his death.
He had been the subject and inspiration of countless ballads and flash songs and he had suggested to Hogarth
the story that linked together his series of pictures "Industry and Idleness." By being put on show by his jailers
he had started that "ridiculous rage of going to Newgate"
deprecated by Walpole, and by bringing to fever pitch an
already intense interest in crime and criminals he had
ensured the success of the "Newgate Pastoral" conceived
by Swift and brought to such lusty life by Gay in *The
Beggar's Opera*.

Within a fortnight of his death the first of the scores
of dramatized versions of the Jack Sheppard story was
performed amidst scenes of great excitement at Drury
Lane. And more than a hundred years later, in 1840,
following the huge success of Harrison Ainsworth's
famous and sensational novel, *Jack Sheppard*, nine new
plays based on the short life of the Newgate hero were
performed in that one year alone.

He was not left only to the attention of dramatists.

Encouraged by Harrison Ainsworth's unprecedented sales, numerous hack novelists and journalists brought out, one after the other in later months, shameless imitations of his melodramatic story. But these imitative and lurid novels, written for readers hungry for violence, degraded Sheppard's character beyond all recognition. Harrison Ainsworth's weak but dashing hero became in later years a monster.

The outrageous exploits of this monster, as described in one of these bloodthirsty novels, had inspired Courvoisier, so he confessed at his trial, to cut the throat of his seventy-two-year old employer Lord William Russell. It was a shocking and well publicized confession. Other crimes, so it was alleged in newspapers and in Parliament, were similarly inspired. Something must be done, the journalists and politicians insisted, about the new wave of crimes of violence and the corruption of imaginative youth. The Lord Chamberlain acting under pressure announced that any further licences to perform plays bearing the name Jack Sheppard in their titles would be refused and that the matter of the books was also being investigated.

But the books still appeared and the licences, it seems, were still granted. And so the damage to Sheppard's name went on and it was permanent. He was towards the end of the century thought of as a stupid and brutal murderer and an inspirer of murderers, and today if he is remembered at all it is as an inhuman and barbarous thief and robber.

He was, of course, nothing of the sort. He was dissolute certainly and he broke the law without regret or repentance. He drank to excess; he spent much of his time in brothels and in the beds of whores; he was subject to fits of furious temper; he was vain and extravagant and self-indulgent and wildly irresponsible; and he became an inveterate and habitual thief. But in a selfish age of violence and cruelty he was neither violent nor cruel, and in an underworld of informers, spies, crimps, and thief-takers he was faithful to his friends to the point of chivalry. Throughout the long agonies of his imprisonment he remained cheerful' and uncomplaining and always, in good times and in bad, he was generous and brave. His intelligence was unquestionable; his technical skill astounding.

He inspired great love and lasting affection not only in his friends but even in those whom he had wronged and who had cause to hate him. In another age and with different opportunities for the satisfaction of his ambitions and appetites and for the release of his bursting energy, he might perhaps, with that quick brain and those sudden spasms of passionate determination, have achieved some manner of greatness.

CHAPTER TWO

THE BACKGROUND

I T CANNOT, it is true, be said of Sheppard that he
was a victim of circumstances. He decided for himself
the pattern of his gay life and the manner of his tragic
death. But the inhumanities of the criminal law and the
customs and conditions of his time were at least partly to
blame for the violence and turbulence of a large part of
the community of which Jack Sheppard was by no means
a unique although a most remarkable example.

During his lifetime and in fact more than a hundred
years after his death every felony, from the stealing of a
watch to being found in the company of gipsies, was
punishable by hanging. It made no difference if the culprit
was young. In 1748 a boy of ten was sentenced to death
and a committee of judges, to whom the case was referred,
decided that "in justice to the public the law should take
its course." It made no difference if the culprit was bullied
into the crime unaware of its significance. In 1777 a

servant girl of fourteen was sentenced to be burned, for the treason of hiding, on instructions from her employer, some farthings whitewashed so that they looked like shillings. It was never for a moment supposed that crime could be prevented by means other than punishment and it was at that time rarely feared that violence might breed violence.

The reformation of criminals and prisoners was not considered either practicable or possible and the first offender was, as often as not, treated with the same cruel severity as the confirmed and hardened ruffian.

If death was a recognized punishment for the most trivial offence, torture under different names and guises was still a frequent preliminary to death and public bestiality a common aftermath. Women could still be sentenced to be laid bare to the waist and publicly whipped and to be burned alive; men found guilty of treason were still disembowelled and their entrails displayed to a fascinated crowd. The white eyeless heads of traitors were still stuck on spikes at Temple Bar and were blown down terrifyingly into the street on a windy night; and the putrefying corpses of highwaymen and pirates were a common sight at cross-roads and along the banks of the Thames, hanging in creaking iron cages suspended from gibbets. Hanging days at Tyburn were a customary public holiday and the condemned men were generally the heroes and the drunken fumbling hangmen the villains of the sensational and revolting drama.

But although it was an age of violence it was, for the privileged few, an age of elegance too.

Passing through the streets, seeing what they wanted to see and ignoring what offended them, were the members of a society quite different from that to which most of the people belonged, the occupants it seemed almost of a different world. They could be seen driving out of the courtyards of their beautiful houses in carriages drawn by six horses, attended by liveried footmen with scented wigs and by decorative black slaves with silver collars round their necks and the marks of the branding iron on their arms. They were those for whom elegance in dress, art, and behaviour was a principal if not an only concern and who confessed themselves ravished by the delicacy and elaborate gracefulness of contemporary European taste in architecture and manners.

This passion for supreme elegance carried into absurdity is exemplified by a set of beaux who, because of their fantastically purposeless and Italianate behaviour, became known as "the macaronis." The macaronis wore their hair in long and scented curls and tripped fastidiously about the more fashionable parts of the town in shoes with perilously high red heels. They generally carried in their beautifully decorated pockets two watches; one, Walpole said, was for telling them what the time was and the other for telling them what the time was not. Their favourite pastime and one at which they spent hour upon hour endeavouring to improve their skill was the whistling of songs through toothpicks. They were, of course, exaggerating the standards of lazy dilettantish behaviour accepted as normal by the members of their class, but not unduly so. They were considered eccentric rather than silly. Few young gentlemen, whether they were macaronis or not, rose early, and a young lady was not usually woken until midday when her little toy of a blackamoor came into her room with a cup of chocolate and brought her pet squirrel or monkey which she fondled while her maid began her long toilet.

A day in the life of an average beau is described by a character in one of Fielding's novels.

"In the morning I arose, took my great stick and walked out in my green frock, with my hair in paper, and sauntered about till ten. Went to the auction; told Lady B. she had a dirty face, laughed heartily at something Captain G. said (I can't remember what, as I did not very well hear it), whispered to Lord ——, bowed to the Duke of ——, and was going to bid for a snuff box, but did not for fear I should have it; two to four dressed myself; four to six dined; six to eight coffee house; eight to nine Drury Lane playhouse; ten to twelve drawing room."

It was a life of ease and frivolity in which the shoes of ladies were not only used as champagne glasses but were, on one occasion at least, eaten fried in butter so that the company could testify "their affection for the lady by eating very heartily of this exquisite impromptu." It was a life in which men drank not so much to the state of drunkenness as to the state of suffocation, and in which there was so little to think about that the gambling fever had taken its natural consequent hold. Vast fortunes were lost night after night at cards; and cards were only one of the many means whereby money was recklessly lost and won. When one day a man fell down outside a London coffee house bets were immediately placed by the customers as to whether he was dead or not. A sympathetic passer-by suggesting that the poor fellow should be bled was shouted down by the punters, as this would, they complained, affect the fairness of the betting.

High society was dedicated to pleasure and it was not ashamed of it. But even in high society violence was only just concealed by the powder and the protocol and kept in uncertain control. Duelling was the outcome of so many minor quarrels that by the end of the century it was considered almost as a national sport. Challenges were made and accepted with just about as much consideration as a man today would give to the acceptance of a pound bet on a round of golf—and this although one or other of the contestants was as likely to be killed as wounded. Indeed in the celebrated duel fought between the Duke of Hamilton and Lord Mohun in 1712 the results were as disastrous as could be expected, for these two noblemen "fought with so violent an animosity that, neglecting the rules of art, they seemed to run on one another, as if they tried who should kill first, in which they were both so unhappily successful that the Lord Mohun was killed outright, and Duke Hamilton died in a few minutes."

This duel, however, was a mild affair compared with that mass contest near the Haymarket reported in *The Weekly Journal* of 21st May 1720, when at about midnight "near 100 gentlemen and others were all engaged at one time...wherein abundance were dangerously wounded; the watchman that came to put an end to the affray was knocked down and barbarously used. At last the patrol of Horse Guards came and finding them obdurate rode through them cutting all their way with their swords."

As an illustration of the extraordinary arguments which ended in duels *The Westminster Journal* in 1735 provides a curious example. It appears that one "Wednesday a duel was fought behind Montagu House between two journeymen lace weavers.... One of the parties discharged his pistol the ball from which took away part of the sleeve of his antagonist's coat, and then like a man of courage without waiting for the fire being returned made the best of his way off the field. The quarrel began at a public house about the mode of cooking a dish of sprats, one insisting on having them fried and the other on having them boiled. With the assistance of some friends, the sum of 3s. was raised to procure the use of pistols to decide this important contest."

For those who did not themselves indulge in these dangerous affrays there were many other violent activities which men could pay to watch and enjoy. There was bull-baiting and bear-baiting and even tiger-baiting; there were men in the pillories to throw mud at and women on the gallows to shout at; there were cock fights and dog fights and prize fights; there were fights between women and fights between bears; and everywhere there was a fight there was gambling and there was drinking.

The newspapers advertised these sporting events in colourful and picturesque phrases.

"At the Royal Cockpit," began a proud announcement of 1700, "will begin a very great cock match, and will continue all the week, wherein most of the considerablest cockers of England are concerned. There will be a battle down upon the pit every day precisely at three o'clock."

The noise in the cockpits was thunderous, as the excited spectators shouted bets and roared abuse and encouragement to the furious contestants on the dirty blood-spattered mat in the pit below them; and when one fight was over and they waited for the next to begin, they uncorked their flasks of brandy or bought pots of gin from the gin seller who was always in attendance. Hanging above them, in a sort of iron basket suspended from the ceiling, there was usually a gambler who was punished in this uncomfortable and ignominious way for not paying his debts, and hung there as a warning to others not to be guilty of the same offence.

On 9th June 1716, *The Weekly Journal* advertised a more uncommon diversion. "At the Bear Garden at Hockley-in-the-Hole at the request of several persons of quality on Monday the eleventh of this instant of June, is one of the largest and most mischievous bears that was ever seen in England to be baited to death, with other variety of Bull-baiting and Bear-baiting; as also a Wild Bull to be turned loose in the Game Place, with fireworks all over him. To begin exactly at three o'clock in the afternoon because the sport continues long."

On Sundays, when the streets and cockpits and prize rings were quieter, there was always Bedlam to visit and the chance of seeing a really horrifying or amusing exhibition of lunacy by the inmates, who were on display there until 1770, when it was felt that the sightseers who paid twopence a head to come in "tended to disturb the tranquillity of the patients" by "making sport and diversion of the miserable inhabitants"; and there were always the free and unofficial fights like the one in the Spa Fields near Islington when "two women fought for a new shift valued at half a guinea. ...The battle was won by Bruising Peg who beat her antagonist in a terrible manner." And for those who had a fancy for the bizarre, there were always the freak shows at "the Commodious Room Opposite the New Inn Surry side of Westminster Bridge where at a shilling each" could be inspected "the Ethiopian Savage. This astonishing animal is of a different species from any ever seen in Europe, and seems to be a link between the Rational and Brute Creation, as he is a striking resemblance of the Human Species. ...Also the Orang Outang..., a calf with eight legs, two tails, two heads and only one body, a very remarkable foreign cat, and an extraordinary exploit done by a white mouse, together with many other curiosities."

These curiosities once included a woman with three breasts who demonstrated her ability to suckle three babies at the same time and who could be persuaded for a fee to perform her remarkable feat at parties which went on all night.

It was a lusty bustling unselfconscious life and a dangerous one. The danger came not only from professional criminals and gangs of amateur hooligans, such as the notorious Mohocks, but from "any foolish drunkard reeling from a feast" who might provoke "a broil and stab you for a jest."

Most gentlemen considered themselves ill dressed without a sword and they wore it not entirely for fashion's sake.

Richard Savage, a young poet and illegitimate son of the Countess of Macclesfield, forced his way with some friends one evening in 1727 into a private room in Robinson's coffee house where a few men were quietly enjoying a game of cards. One of Savage's friends walked up to the table and, insultingly eyeing the players, all of whom were strangers to him, kicked it over. "What do you mean by that?" asked one of the players. "What do *you* mean?" said Savage and ran the man through the chest with his sword. Savage was found guilty of murder but was pardoned. It was not an exceptional case.

A young gentleman named Plunkett, when going to the shop of a wig-maker to collect a wig which he had ordered, was asked to pay rather more than he had expected. He haggled over the price but the wig maker refused to come down more than a guinea and Plunkett, picking up a razor which he had noticed lying on the counter, cut the old man's throat from ear to ear.

Senseless murders such as these were not in the least uncommon. Tempers were easily lost, passions were ungovernable. A quarrel might end in murder or an argument in a riot. Riots indeed were almost as common as murders.

Soldiers rioted against their Hanover shirts; footmen rioted when they were stopped from going to the theatre; workmen rioted when Irish labourers undertook to work for less money than they. There were Gin Riots and High Church Riots and Corn Riots and they were all serious affairs. In the Spitalfields Riots of 1719, when four thousand weavers marched through London molesting all women wearing Indian linen or calico and throwing ink at them, more lives were lost than the Government cared to admit; and in the Gordon Riots at least two hundred and eighty-five people were killed, excluding those who drank themselves to death on the raw spirits which flowed through the streets when Langdale's distillery was burned down, and excluding the twenty-one people who were subsequently hanged for their part in the havoc.

The reasons for a riot were of little concern to the mob, which joined in for the fun or for the looting, the chances of free drink or free women, or perhaps free food for starving families.

As soon as an angry crowd collected on any pretence whatsoever, it was only a matter of minutes before a man appeared to give it some direction and purpose, either for his own gain, or for a few hours of idle amusement like the early morning hours spent one day by Charles Fox when he with "Lord Derby and his brother, Major Stanley, and two or three more young men of quality, having been drinking at Almack's, suddenly thought of making a tour of the streets and were joined by the Duke of Ancaster, who was very drunk . . . and had been breaking windows. Finding the mob before Palisser's house some of the young lords said, 'Why don't you break Lord Germaine's windows?' The populace had been so little tutored that they asked who he was, and being encouraged, broke his windows."

Foreigners came in for the worst treatment at the hands of the mob. Frenchmen (and most foreigners were referred to as Frogs whatever their nationality) and Jews were pelted and insulted in the street for no cause at all other than that they were not English. And if a foreigner committed some crime against an Englishman the anger of the mob was ferocious. A Portuguese sailor who stabbed an English sailor in the back after an argument in Whitechapel was nailed "by his ear to the wall. Some time after he broke from there with the loss of part of it and ran; but the mob was so incensed that they followed out and wounded him with knives till at last he either fell or threw himself into a puddle of water where he died."

A Jew, who was believed to have picked the pocket of a sailor and who as a punishment for his supposed crime underwent "the usual discipline of ducking, hopped out of the water pretending to have his leg broke and was carried off by some of his brethren. But the sailors discovering the trick," pursued him with reinforcements to his house in Duke's Place, a Jewish quarter, which they attacked and entering the houses "threw everything they met with out of the window, broke the glasses, tore the beds and ripped up the wainscot leaving the house in the most ruinous condition. With the furniture three children sick of the small pox were thrown out."

Children grew up learning to expect such treatment. The nation's conscience did not concern itself with the helpless young before Thomas Coram, that great old sea-captain so lovingly and faithfully painted by Hogarth, began the humane work which was one of the turning-points of the social history of the eighteenth century.

Unwanted babies were left out in the streets to die or were strangled and thrown onto dung heaps or into open drains. Those few that survived were an irksome charge upon the parish and were put out to gin-sodden parish nurses who were known to maim them or to disfigure them in some way, so that when they were old enough to go out begging they might by exciting pity be the more successful. These nurses made further profit out of their charges by hiring them out to beggars at fourpence a day; but if a baby appeared too sickly to survive and thus become an ultimate source of profit to its nurse, it was soon dispatched by "the infernal monster" who would "throw a spoonful of gin down the child's throat which instantly strangles the babe." When the searchers come to inspect the body and enquire what distemper caused death, it is answered "convulsions."

When the parish child was old enough to leave the nurse and go out into the world, and quite often six or seven was considered a suitable age, he was bound as an apprentice to some dangerous or noxious trade which found it otherwise difficult to get labour and into which no boy from a decent family would be permitted to go.

Having got his fee out of the parish an unscrupulous master would then endeavour to get rid of the boy so that he might earn another fee by taking a second apprentice. Many masters took several more apprentices than they could possibly hope to teach or find work for, and then starved them or maltreated them so that they died or ran away. There are numerous cases of inhuman cruelty to parish children on record, but convictions were rare and punishments light. No wonder that the poor little apprentices, as terrified of the master they had come to as of the nurse they had left, without guidance, education, love, or care ran out into the world to begin

a life of crime that seemed the only means of escape from
the terrible degradation of an existence in which they
could see no hope for the future and no end to the
monotony, bitterness, and interminable cruelty of the
present.

Once on the streets they were, if they looked old
enough, in constant danger of the press gang, or of
kidnappers on the look out for likely-looking lads to sell
to a ship captain ready to sail to the American colonies
or to India.

Legally only seamen could be impressed, but during a
"hot press" anyone found wandering in the streets or
idling in the gin shops or taverns, particularly those close
to the river, was grist to the mill. Brothels were frequently visited by well-armed press gangs, and one
"Friday night a press gang having received intelligence
of a house near Poplar where the thieves skulk till the
evening . . . went very unexpectedly and surrounded the
house from which they took 17 and carried them away to
the tender at the Tower."

The crimps representing the East India Company and
the American plantations were even more widely feared
and were certainly more wholeheartedly unscrupulous in
their methods. A revealing and probably accurate account
of the activities of one gang of these vultures is given in
The British Gazette, which describes a "horrid scene near
Leicester Fields" where a "young lad on Wednesday
evening was perceived running from thence towards the

Haymarket, and two or three fellows crying after him, 'Stop thief!' Some of the passengers no sooner stopped him as such than he told them he was no thief, but had been kidnapped by his pursuers, who had chained him in a cellar with about nine more in order to be shipped off for India, and that he had made his escape so far by mere desperation, swearing he would run the first through with a pen knife he held open in his hand. The youth was instantly liberated, and the whole fury of the populace fell upon his kidnapping pursuers, one of whom was heartily ducked in the Mews pond. All the remaining youths were taken from the place of confinement by the intervention of the populace. These robbers of human flesh, it seems, not only intoxicate country lads till they can confine them but have been known to stop people in the streets and carry them to their horrid dens, under the various pretences of their being deserters, pickpockets, etc. They likewise attend register offices, and hire youths there for servants, whom they immediately confine, and sell them either to the military or to the India kidnapping contractors."

The London in which these "horrid scenes" took place had been rapidly rebuilt after the devastation of the Great Fire, but it was still in 1720 a relatively small place, comprising the cities of London and Westminster, the Borough of Southwark, and several small and scarcely connected parishes. There were still open fields just north of what is now Oxford Street and south of St. James's Square. Bayswater, Chelsea, and Paddington were still small country hamlets. Vegetables grown in market gardens at Lambeth were hawked about the streets and dairy maids brought in cows from the farms around Kensington to sell their milk from door to door in the town.

The metropolis, as it was generally called, was a place of extraordinary contrasts.

In the prosperous commercial parts of the town the noise, the colours, and the bustle were wonderful. Many of the streets in spite of the fire were still very narrow and the creaking sign boards hanging outside many houses instead of a number, as well as outside every shop and tavern, sometimes touched each other overhead. Beneath these boards the scurrying life of the streets went on. Carriages, horses, sedan chairs, and carts rattled their way past each other over the cobbles and splashed through the pools of mud. A row of stone posts marked the edge of the street and the beginning of the pavement and rough and tumble sedan-chairmen, although prohibited by statute from walking behind the posts, rushed headlong down the space intended for pedestrians, knocking them over into doorways or under the clanging iron rim of a cartwheel.

Having stepped into a muddy pool out of the way of a chairman, a pedestrian might pass under a window as a maid emptied the contents of a chamber pot on his head or pass by a door as a housewife flung out a bucketful of potato peelings. A barber shaking a wig out of his shop window might cover him with powder and a passing chimney sweeper cover him with soot. He might even have his hat and wig snatched from his head by a little boy hiding in a bread basket on the head of a tough and surly-looking baker. Pickpockets jostled him on every side and twelve-year-old prostitutes accosted him. Street robbers watched him contemplatively from side streets. At the tops of their raucous voices street vendors shouted in his ears their varied wares, from oysters to taffity tarts and from patent medicines made from hogs' lice to ginger biscuits and barley broth; and on the doorsteps of shops apprentices bawled at him a list of the things their masters had for sale within.

Beyond the topsy-turvy roof-tops he could see the spires and domes of new churches and the rising stone façades of new houses, the churches of Wren, the elegant porticos and "Heroic" colonnades of Vanbrugh, and the baroque extravagancies of Hawksmoor. This recent and impressive style in architecture still thrilled those who had the taste and leisure to admire it. But behind this grace and beauty, far in spirit if not in distance from the symmetrical gardens of William Kent and the fanciful fountains of Lord Burlington, unnoticed by the rich and sparkling, witty, bored, and carefree members of polite society, were the underprivileged and underfed poor, crowded into the toppling teeming slums of Shoreditch

and Spitalfields and St. Giles's. Here the crumbling tenements seemed as remote from the palatial houses of the
ruling class as from the busy shops and offices of the
tradespeople and businessmen.

Surrounding the tenement houses in these slums were
the numerous gin shops and brothels and the filthy doss-
houses into which for a penny a night were admitted
beggars, prostitutes, children, and drunken labourers to
sleep, regardless of age or sex, and as many as twenty
in a small room, on the lousy rat-ridden straw.

Refuse and excrement and dead animals were thrown
out of doors and left in the stinking alleyways and courtyards to rot and putrefy in the sun or to be washed by the
rain, which poured down in streams from the broken
gutters on the roof-tops, into the open trough that ran
down most streets to serve as a drain. The Fleet ditch
into which many of these subsidiary street drains flowed,
and which was used by all the most noxious trades as a
refuse pit, was an abominable sewer the stench from which
was indescribable. The Fleet was not only full of dead
dogs but was also occupied by hogs which fattened themselves there in the filth and stagnant slime and came up
on occasions to wander about the streets. "A fatter boar
was hardly ever seen than the one taken up" one day in
1736 "coming out of the Fleet ditch," where it had been,
so its owner claimed, for five months.

The streets in these slum areas were of course unlighted and rarely paved, the statutory obligation imposed

upon the householders to pave the streets immediately opposite their own houses being haphazardly enforced. And the houses, which were built higgledy-piggledy in packed confusion and were used during the daytime as airless overcrowded workshops and factories, were leaking verminous habitations, a danger to health and limb alike. Doctor Johnson observed as a young man that a common sound in London was the crash of a falling building, and on one occasion a boy running breathless into a house sent the whole family rushing helter-skelter out of doors as they immediately presumed the roof was falling in. Contemporary newspapers described these frequent crashes of bricks and mortar with regularity. "An old lodging house," ran one such report in 1728, "in Plumtree Court Broad Street St. Giles's fell down, by which accident seven poor wretches were crushed to death, and many were desperately maimed. There being other houses in the court in like tottering condition, the mob assembled in a few days afterwards and pulled them down."

A house was invariably divided into tenements, the owners of the property living usually on the top floor with the poorest tenants in the basement, the rooms between being let off separately and those on the higher levels commanding better rents and being occupied by more respectable tenants than those on the lower floors. The garret was often occupied by poor apprentices and shop boys who lay down to sleep on boards and straw

mattresses placed across the roof joists. During the daytime a few bricks were pulled out of the wall to let in the
light, when there were no windows, and were stuffed
back again with rags to fill up the cracks during the cold
night.

It was in the cellars, however, that the most pitiful
squalor was to be found. Here whole families lay in the
fetid atmosphere and played cards by candlelight or
drank the coarse gin which was distilled and sold so
cheaply. In some cellars, particularly in those occupied
by poor Irish labourers and vagrants, pigs and sometimes
even asses, in spite of a statute of William III, were to
be found living in the same dark cramped quarters as
their human owners.

A cellar although occupied as a home by one or two
families and their animals might also be at the same time
a gin shop, and throughout the night, while children
slept and hogs grunted and old men murmured in their
dreams, the customers were served in the uncertain
flickering light and the drinking and cursing and quarrelling went on. Nearby perhaps "houses which are running
to ruin are filled with beggars, some of whom are asleep
while others are pulling down the timber and packing it
up to sell to washerwomen and clear starchers," who
started work at one o'clock in the morning.

The working day began early for those who had work
to do and working hours were long. Wages were low
and were fixed without particular relevance to the cost

of living. A labourer was paid about ten shillings a week before 1765 and a journeyman earned between thirteen and fifteen shillings although, of course, in certain circumstances and in very skilled trades a hard-working man might earn as much as three or even four pounds a week.* But work was always very uncertain and in bad times poor relief was casual and inadequate. During the depression of the weaving trade in 1719 hundreds of weavers' families were existing in a starving condition on less than ten pence a day. And to do this with rent at possibly three shillings a week, coarse beef at fourpence a pound and diluted milk at fivepence a quart was difficult, and for some families impossible. The little-varied diet, of adults and children alike, in hard times could be not much more than stale bread and small beer twice a day. Starvation was not uncommon.

In circumstances such as these and with only a few unpaid and corrupt constables and decrepit old watchmen to uphold the law, it is not surprising that there was so much crime and violence. While unemployment and uncertainty of work were accepted as inevitable hazards of everyday life, there were always bound to be many people who lived partly by crime and on the edge of the criminal class. Once caught the severity of the punishments for

*An excellent picture of the conditions of life and work of the poor in eighteenth-century London is given by M. Dorothy George in *London Life in the Eighteenth Century* (Kegan Paul, Trench, Trubner & Co. Ltd., 1925, reprinted by the London School of Economics, 1951).

young delinquents and for those who were guilty of a sudden desperate lapse, together with the atrocious conditions in the overcrowded prisons, did much to ensure that the first offender soon became a hardened criminal.

It was not yet expected that life could be anything other than hard and insecure for the weak and the unprotected. And yet amidst the squalor and the degradation, the fear and the insecurity, men lived quiet honest lives and brought up children in decency if not in comfort. It was a struggle for the very poor to live by honest means alone, but it was possible and it was done. In the worst and poorest districts there were good hard-working parents striving to make a decent home for their children in a selfish hostile world and to give them a better chance in life than they had had themselves.

It was into such a family as this that Jack Sheppard was born.

CHAPTER THREE

BOYHOOD &
APPRENTICESHIP

———

HIS father was a carpenter, a poor and rather sickly man who made, as his father and grandfather had done before him, an honest and precarious living in White's Row, Spitalfields, the centre of the London weaving industry and a ragged sprawling slum between Bishopsgate and Bethnal Green. Jack was born in the Sheppards' lodgings in White's Row in March 1702. He was a tiny feeble baby and neither the midwife nor his parents expected him to survive. They had just lost their previous baby and their eldest son Thomas was a difficult moody child. There was, the parents believed, a bad strain in their blood, and with the intention of invoking the help of his Maker the new baby was taken, the day after he was born, to be baptised at St. Dunstan's, Stepney, where prayers might be said for his survival.

He was christened John after the baby that had died, and as soon as the service was over his father carried him back quickly, wrapped up in a blanket, to the little house in Spitalfields.

A year or two later Mr. Sheppard collapsed at his work-bench and never recovered consciousness. His widow was left alone to fend as best she could for her two sons and the baby daughter who had just been born to her. When Jack was six, however, his sister died, and as his mother felt no longer able to keep up a home, she went out to domestic service with a Mr. Kneebone who kept a draper's shop at the sign of the Angel in the Strand, and Jack was sent at the expense of the parish to the work-house school in Bishopsgate Street, to begin his meagre education. What happened to the elder brother is obscure*, but it seems likely that he had already by this time left home of his own accord and had joined a gang of street boys "sleeping in the ashes and dealing always in the street dirt...wicked as the devil could desire to have them be at so early an age and ripe for all the other parts of mischief that suited them as they advanced in years."

Mr. Garrett's school near Great St. Helen's in Bishopsgate Street, where the six-year-old Jack now began to learn how to read and write, was considered by the parish officers as a place where education was dispensed purely as a necessary and irksome preliminary to apprentice-

---

*He was at one time thought to have been apprenticed to a noble family as a foot boy.

ship. Workhouse schools were a charge upon the parish funds, and the parish officers were criticized for doing less than their duty if they did not keep the expenses of these schools down to the absolute minimum.

Consequently they were greatly overcrowded and understaffed and the food was poor and often inadequate. About forty children slept in a single room under the gin-bleary eyes of a harridan who was responsible for their spiritual welfare and bodily health and cleanliness. Wooden bunks were arranged in tiers around the walls, and in the better-managed schools each child shared his bed with a friend and had "a pair of sheets, two blankets and a rugg." In most schools, however, sleeping conditions were far worse and as many as eight dirty, unkempt, and hungry children were crowded together under a single flea-ridden blanket. In a school in Shoreditch thirty-nine children were once found by a visitor lying cramped together in a wooden three-tiered bunk.

The day began at half past five or six with prayers and the church catechism which a child was expected to have by heart before he left to be apprenticed. Breakfast followed at half past six, and all morning between seven and twelve the children were set to work on some task such as sewing or shoe mending, or spinning wool or knitting stockings, and were called out about twenty or thirty at a time for an hour's reading or writing or perhaps a little arithmetic. Dinner was at twelve and after this they could spend a short time at play, but only a short time, as the work at their looms and lasts must go on, for the finances of the school to a certain extent depended on it. The work continued until six o'clock when they were sent off with a piece of bread and lard to their uncomfortable beds.

The age at which they left school to begin their apprenticeship depended to a large extent upon the demand for apprentices in any particular trade and upon the state of the finances of the parish. Few parishes could afford to apprentice poor children to a clean or skilled trade in which fees of fifteen or even thirty pounds were required and obtained. And if a parish could afford these fees it was unwilling to waste its money when a child could equally well be disposed of for five pounds or even less.

It was, therefore, an almost invariable rule for a parish child to be apprenticed as a servant if she were a girl and if he were a boy to some cheap and undesirable trade which could not afford to pick and choose its apprentices or to demand a high fee for training them. A likely trade for a parish boy was that of chimney sweeping, which would take a child at even four years old as a climbing boy. The fees would certainly not be more than five pounds and the smaller and thinner the child the better.

The chimney sweepers' trade always needed more apprentices than any other, not only because climbing boys grew up and became too big for their job, but also because their death rate was so high. A master chimney sweeper giving evidence before a parliamentary commit-

tee, appointed in 1788 to consider a bill for the protection
of apprentices, said that many boys he had known went
for as many as five years without once washing and died
before they were released from their apprenticeship of
"sooty warts" or chimney-sweepers' cancer.

An apprentice was usually bound until he was twenty-
four, although by 1767 the age had been lowered to
twenty-one, and during the years of his apprenticeship
he was obliged to work hard and long. Average hours in
most trades were from six in the morning until six at
night with perhaps an hour at the most for dinner between
twelve and one. He worked all day on Saturdays and the
only holidays he could expect, apart from Sundays, were
three days at Christmas, Easter, and Whitsun, although
he might get an extra day off when there was an execution
at Tyburn, as little work was done on the day of a hanging.

His happiness, of course, to a great extent depended
upon the treatment he received at the hands of his master.
And the masters, as the contemporary Sessions Papers
show, were as likely to be cruel as to be kind.

The public conscience and the law were weighted
heavily in their favour. An employer who was responsible
for the death of a parish apprentice was rarely found
guilty of murder and was unlucky to be convicted of manslaughter. There were precedents enough indeed for an
acquittal and a murdering employer on trial for his life
could confidently expect to be exonerated from all blame.
The fact that such trials were not uncommon is a sure

indication that cruelty to parish apprentices was widespread; for there can be no doubt that for every case which came into the courts there were ten that should have done and for every cruel employer convicted there were more than a hundred who were not.

A certain measure of severity was expected in the treatment of a poor apprentice and the line between severity and cruelty is difficult to define. And so it was that the employer got away with murder, because murder was often interpreted as an accident for which an idle apprentice had only himself to blame. No such advantages in the interpretation of the law were, however, made available to the unprotected apprentice. A little girl apprentice of nine was sentenced to death in 1735 for stealing some money from her mistress and running away with it; and there are many other similar cases in the Sessions Papers.

It was not until the late 1760's that the first steps were taken to improve the conditions of the neglected and ill-treated parish child. Public opinion had by then been roused by two cases which were widely reported in the Press and which because of their exceptional brutality and sordidness did much to bring the plight of the poor apprentice to the notice of social reformers and to Parliament. The murderers in both these cases were condemned to death, but similar bestiality earlier on in the century—of which there is so much evidence—might well have resulted only in a charge of manslaughter.

The first of the two cases concerned a Mrs. Brownrigg, a midwife whose husband had a plumber's business in Fleet Street. Mrs. Brownrigg was well known as a cruel mistress from whom two parish apprentices had already run away, when Mary Clifford was bound to her by the parish officers of Whitefriars, who either made no inquiries about the infamous woman or who preferred to ignore the reports they received.

The new apprentice was beaten savagely and without cause as soon as she entered the house and this treatment continued the whole time she was there. She was made to sleep on straw in the coal cellar and was constantly perished with cold and close to starvation. One day, unable to stand any longer the pangs of hunger which a long diet of bread and water had induced, she broke into a food cupboard. Mrs. Brownrigg caught her as she stretched up to reach the tempting food, and stripping her naked she lashed furiously at her with the butt end of a whip. Then, bleeding and in agony, the poor girl was sent back to the cellar with a chain tightened to the point of suffocation round her neck and her hands tied behind her back.

A few days later, after she had complained to a lodger in the house of the inhumanity with which she and her fellow apprentices were treated, Mrs. Brownrigg rushed at her brandishing a pair of scissors and cut through her tongue in two places.

It was some time, however, before a neighbour who

had heard the ceaseless screams and groans emanating from Mr. Brownrigg's house thought that perhaps the apprentices there were "treated with unwarrantable severity." His maidservant reported that, anxious to know what happened in the locked and forbidding house, she had peeped through a skylight and had seen one apprentice filthily dirty and in rags kept in a covered yard with a pig.

An overseer of the poor was at last instructed to go to the house and demand to see Mary Clifford. Mrs. Brownrigg produced another apprentice instead, who was taken to the workhouse and there, after her clothes had been painfully removed from her scarred and bloody back and after she had been assured that she would not be taken back to Fleet Street, she told her pitiable story. A search in the house was then made for the real Mary Clifford, who was at length found hidden in a cupboard in the dining-room. Her condition when she was taken to St. Bartholomew's Hospital was "impossible to describe. Nearly her whole body was ulcerated." She died within a few days.

Mrs. Brownrigg was tried and hanged for murder. Her husband, who had evidently encouraged her brutalities, and her son, who had helped her to perpetrate them, were each sentenced to six months' imprisonment.

The second terrible example of the cruelty with which many parish apprentices were treated and of the power which their employers were given over them was pro-

vided by the case of Mrs. Meteyard, which was published
in the Press the following year.

Mrs. Meteyard and her daughter kept a millinery
shop in Bruton Street, Berkeley Square, and employed as
servants and shop girls five parish apprentices. One of
these girls, Anne Taylor, was apparently not in good
health and, being unable to do as much work as her fellow
apprentices, she was constantly beaten and abused for her
laziness by her employers. Feeling that she could no
longer bear this ill-treatment she ran away, but she was
soon caught and brought back to the shop, where she was
locked up in an attic on a diet of bread and water. Once
again she escaped and once more she was brought back to
her tormentors, who this time thought that the time had
come to punish her properly. After being flogged mer-
cilessly with a broom handle she was tied up to the door
of a back room and kept there for the rest of the day. For
three days as soon as she had got out of bed she was tied
up to this door "without food or drink" and left there,
unable to sit down or kneel or in any way to take the
weight of her body off her legs, until it was dark, when
she was allowed to crawl up to bed again. On the third
night she was so weak she could scarcely summon the
strength to drag her pain-wracked body up the stairs to
bed. The following day she was obviously close to death.
As an encouragement to harder work and as an object
lesson in the wages of laziness, the other four apprentices
were brought down to watch her agony. Towards the

middle of the day it became obvious that the poor child was dead and one of the other apprentices ran to Miss Meteyard to tell her that Anne had stopped moving. Miss Meteyard said she'd soon move her and hit her over the head with a shoe. But as this did not appear to arouse her, she cut her down from the door and in vain tried to revive her with smelling salts.

When they were satisfied that the girl was dead Miss Meteyard and her mother carried the body up into a garret and locked it in. They then gave out that the intractable Anne Taylor had absconded once more and nobody disbelieved them. The other apprentices who knew that she was dead were too terrified to say so and Anne's sister, who was heard to make some remark as to the manner of her death, was immediately murdered too. The remaining apprentices went about their work in silent terror.

After two months the Meteyards, fearing that the smell of decomposition in the garret was getting strong enough to be noticed in the shop, cut up the body and having burned what they could, "cursing the unhappy creature because her bones were so long consuming," stuffed the remaining pieces into an open gully-hole. And there they remained until a constable found them. Thinking that they had come from a nearby dissecting-room he had them buried.

Four years later the daughter left home after a violent quarrel with her mother and it was as a result of a subsequent quarrel in which they shouted accusations at each other that they were arrested and brought to trial.

Both were sentenced to death, and the mother on the morning of her execution had a fit as she was put into the cart and when hanged at Tyburn she was still unconscious.

Jack was lucky when the time came for him to leave the workhouse school in Bishopsgate that he had a mother who cared for him and who had character enough to insist that he should not run the risk of being apprenticed to a household such as the Meteyards' or the Brownriggs'. She persuaded Mr. Kneebone, the kindly linen draper who was her employer, to take him on as a shop boy, and Jack in 1710, when he was eight years old, came to live with his mother at Mr. Kneebone's shop in the Strand.

For both the mother and the son the next seven years were happy ones. Mr. Kneebone was a generous and contented man and grew as fond of the cheerful intelligent little boy as he apparently was of Mrs. Sheppard. When the shop was closed he would help Jack to improve his reading and writing and would write out, in his careful tradesman's hand, words and sentences for Jack to copy. And when he knew that the time had come for Jack to go out into the world, he induced an acquaintance of his whom he knew would be kind to the boy to take him on as an apprentice.

The acquaintance was Owen Wood, a carpenter and house joiner in Wych Street, and Jack, who was now fifteen, was apprenticed to him for seven years, on condition that Wood was given the job of doing the joinery for Kneebone's country house at Hampstead which the draper was at that time just about to build. With this contract safely in his pocket Wood waived any rights he had to the usual apprenticeship fee and Jack moved into the third-floor garret in Wych Street which was to be his home for the next six years.

During this time Jack proved himself a good pupil with a quick and resourceful mind. He soon became a skilled craftsman and a locksmith of exceptional ability.

CHAPTER FOUR

BAD COMPANY

—

ITS at The Black Lion tavern in Newton Street,
Drury Lane, that the story really begins. Here it was
that Jack after a hard day's work at Mr. Wood's in
Wych Street began some time in the spring of 1723 to
spend his evenings and to acquire a taste for brandy and
for the company of whores.

The Black Lion was one of numerous taverns in the
neighborhood of Covent Garden and Drury Lane that
was as much a brothel as a "boosing ken."* Not so
fashionable as Tom King's coffee house in Covent Garden
nor so famous as The Rose, near the Drury Lane Theatre,
in Russell Street, it had much in common with both; the
same debauched abandoned women were here, the same
cursing rowdy wild-eyed drunkenness, the same atmosphere of uninhibited pleasure and intermittently

---

*A Swiss traveller in London, César de Saussure, noticed that those
coffee houses which were also "temples of Venus" had as a hanging
sign "a woman's arm or hand holding a coffee pot."

controlled violence. But the customers at The Black Lion were more wholeheartedly vicious, more generally criminal than at Tom King's, where the company was at least mixed and where "the chimney sweeper, the pick-pocket and maudlin peer were often to be seen in the same seat together." For it was one of the charms of Moll King that she would serve with the same apparent cheerfulness and rough affection "gardeners and market people in common with her Lords of the Knighted Rank."

The presence of peers and men of fashion, however, did not of course prevent the sudden outbreaks of violence which were common to all these bawdy drinking houses. In Hogarth's vivid and evocative impression of Covent Garden at seven o'clock of a winter's morning, through the open door of Tom King's, "a kind of Low Hutt rather than an edifice," can be seen a group of early morning revellers brawling. They fight with drawn swords in the doorway, thus hiding the indecent picture of a monk and a nun which hangs on the wall within.

At The Rose in spite of the employment of a tough porter the customers were no less violent. Although in the daytime respectable enough, The Rose became at night one of the most wild and dangerous taverns in London, "where murderous assaults were frequently occurring amongst the bullies of the time."* It had a reputation

*A fascinating account of The Rose and other Covent Garden taverns and coffee houses is given by Peter Quennell in *Hogarth's Progress* (Viking, 1955).

for *divertimenti* which no other London brothel could equal. The most innocent of these amusements was provided by the porter himself who was called "Leathercoat" and who for the price of a drink would lie down in the street while a carriage ran over his chest. After his death "Leathercoat" was dissected by Doctor Hunter and "the appearance of muscular strength was extraordinary both in form of the muscles and in the remarkable processes of bones into which they were inserted."

More extravagant *exhibitions* than those given by the porter were provided inside the house, where the "posture woman" enticingly took off her clothes to perform her "feats of indecent activity." Having undressed she lay naked on her back on an enormous pewter plate, her knees drawn up to her chin, her hands clasped under her thighs in the attitude of a trussed chicken, while around the plate the drunken spectators, both men and women, played a game which is perhaps better imagined than described. Another game was played around the posture woman with a lighted candle, the destination of which, as a French observer delicately put it, *il suffit de vous laisser à diviner.*

Such excitements as these were provided at most of the innumerable taverns in the neighborhood which even before the end of the seventeenth century was becoming to be considered no longer a fashionable address. As the polite society gradually moved out, the brothel keepers moved in, buying up the still impressive buildings and turning them over to a variety of purposes. Every brothel was an open drinking house and most taverns had their back and upper rooms, where in the smoky sweaty candle-lit atmosphere the whoring and drinking and gambling went on all night. Already by 1721 there were more than twenty known gambling dens in the Covent Garden district alone and no one knew how many brothels or drinking cellars.

For the more perverted tastes there were other establishments, the scene in one of which was described in Jonathan Wild's account of the activities of the City Marshal.

One night [apparently] the Marshal invited his man, the Bucklemaker, to a house near the end of the Old Bailey, telling him he would introduce him to a company of He-Whores. The man, not rightly apprehending his meaning, asked him if they were hermaphrodites.—'No, ye fool you' [said the Marshal] 'they are sodomites, such as deal with their own sex, instead of females.' This being a curiosity the Buckle-maker had not yet met with, he willingly accompanied his master to the house, which they had no sooner entered, but the Marshal was complimented by the company with the title of Madam and Ladyship. The man asking the occasion of these uncommon devoirs, the Marshal said it was a familiar language peculiar to the house. The man was not long there before he was more surprized than at first. The men calling one another 'my dear,' and hugging, kissing, and tickling each other, as if they were a mixture of wanton males and females, and assuming effem-

inate voices and airs. Some telling others that they ought to
be whipped for not coming to school more frequently. The
Marshal was very merry in this assembly, and dallied with
the young sparks with a great deal of pleasure, till some
persons came into the house that he had little expected to
meet with in that place; and then finding it out of his power
to secure the lads to himself, he started up on a sudden in a
prodigious rage, asking the frolicking youths, if they were
become so common as to use these obnoxious houses, and
telling them he would spoil their diversion; upon this he
made his exit with his man. As he was going out of the house,
he said, he supposed they would have the impudence to make
a ball. The man desiring him to explain what he meant by
that, he answered, there was a noted house in Holborn, to
which such sort of persons used to repair, and dress themselves
up in women's apparel, and dance and romp about, and make
such a hellish noise, that a man would swear they were a parcel
of cats a catterwouling—'But', says he,'I'll be revenged of
these smock-faced young dogs. I'll watch their waters, and
secure 'em, and send 'em to the Compter.'*

The quantity of spirits drunk in these brothels and taverns and in the workshops and houses and in the streets was
enormous. Hogarth's"GinLane,"extravagant and appalling as it appears, was not considered exaggerated by his
contemporaries.The principal characters and details of
scene were indeed, as in most of his pictures, taken from
life.

*"An answer to a libel, entitled A Discovery of the conduct of
receivers and thief-takers in London...written by C——s H——n
wherein is prov'd who is originally the Grand Thief-Taker, etc." (1718).

The scene is St. Giles's, the slum quarter known as "the rookery," to the east of what is now Oxford Circus. In the background beyond the edges of the slum, "the licenced Alsatia of beggary and wretchedness," is the spire of Hawksmoor's recently finished church St. George's, Bloomsbury, emphasizing by its rather elaborate and ornate richness the ramshackle ugliness and degradation below. The central figure in the picture is a bedraggled woman who sprawls half-naked at the top of a flight of steps, staring in front of her with an expression on her drunken face of senseless and grotesque amusement as she reaches for a pinch of snuff. A baby till lately suckling at her flaccid breast falls helpless and unregarded onto the cobblestones beneath. By her white and scabrous legs sits a corpse-like ballad-seller leaning back exhausted against a wooden rail, his great sunken eyelids shadowed by the nearness of death. "Buy my ballads," the poor wretch who served Hogarth as a model for this character used to croak, "and I will give you a glass of gin for nothing."

Above him in the street are other victims of Gin Royal; the men brawling in front of the distillery, the women selling their kitchenware to the pawnbroker, the little charity girls sipping, the baby choking, the starving man gnawing at a dog's bone. A young woman is laid into her coffin; in a garret dangles a man who has hanged himself; a nearby house topples and begins to fall. The sordid gin cellar bears over the doorway the well-known legend:

Drunk for a penny
Dead drunk for two pennies
Clean straw for nothing.

It is a terrible admonitory picture. But warnings such
as these were unheeded and the drinking went on. Parish
nurses gave gin to their charges to keep them quiet,
children drank it, employers sold it to their workmen,
servant girls and shop boys were given a glass when they
were sent to the chandler's shop to buy the groceries.

It was on sale everywhere. It was sold in the dram
shops, of which by 1722 there were nearly seven thousand
in the cities of London and Westminster alone; it was
sold in the ale houses, in the prisons, and in the streets,
and by practically every shopkeeper in business. A
committee of justices reported that "chandlers, many
tobacconists, and such who sell fruit or herbs in stalls and
wheelbarrows sell Geneva. . . . In the hamlet of Bethnal
Green above forty weavers sell it."

The invitation to get drunk for a penny on a quarter of
a pint of gin was openly accepted. The bodies of men and
women and children could be seen lying dead drunk where
they had fallen, in the middle of the day as well as at night,
in many of the streets of the slum quarters of St. Giles's
and Whetstone Park. In the gin cellars rows of bodies sat
propped up against the wall until the effects of the spirit
should wear off and they could start drinking again. By
1736 it was estimated that one house in every six in Lon-

don was a gin shop and in 1751, when the worst years
were over, Fielding was still warning that "should the
drinking this poison be continued in its present height
during the next twenty years, there will be by that time
few of the common people left to drink it," and that "gin
is the principal sustenance (if it may be so called) of more
than a hundred thousand people in the metropolis. . . .
The intoxicating draught itself disqualifies them from
any honest means to acquire it, at the same time that it
removes sense of fear and shame and emboldens them to
commit every wicked and desperate enterprise."

Certainly in the first half of the century the death rate
and the crime rate had risen alarmingly. The population
of London scarcely increased at all during the period and
while gin was not wholly responsible doctors believed
even after the Act of 1751 that one-eighth of the deaths
of adults in London could be attributed to the excessive
drinking of spirits.

But reform was slow to come. Previous efforts to stop
the poor from drinking gin had been half-hearted and the
various Acts designed to restrict consumption had had
little or no effect. In a Parliament largely occupied and
ultimately governed by landowners dedicated to the
principles of *laisser-faire* and self-aggrandizement it was
difficult if not impossible to pass any measures which
interfered with agricultural interests. The money derived
by the farmers and landowners from the distillation of
spirits from English grain was an important source of

their income. While there was a good market for corn, agricultural interests were secure. What else, they asked, was there that mattered?

So in these early years of the century the gin flowed unchecked from the distilleries. About four million gallons were drunk each year. Wretchedness and poverty, crime and disease increased at an alarming rate; and starving families sent out their children into the unlit streets, their little boys as beggars and their daughters to join the growing procession of prostitutes.

The eighteenth-century prostitute was more often than not a pathetic little ill-clad figure whose body could be hired for sixpence. Most of them were less than eighteen years old, many only twelve. They were mainly recruited from the large number of servant children, illegitimate parish apprentices, beggar girls, and other unfortunates who had run away from the cruelties of a brutal mistress, or who had been tempted by a plausible procuress into a brothel and there initiated by a rough habitué or the son of the house into their new profession. They were kept on the staff only so long as they remained reasonably healthy, but when the symptoms of a veneral disease had become obvious they were thrown out of doors to fend for themselves.

Once on the streets a girl was not likely to earn a living by prostitution alone, and when her solicitations were successful her hands were in her customer's pockets as soon as he had his arms around her and was unlikely to notice her prying fingers. If she was caught, justice was dealt out with haphazard carelessness by a magistrate who decided for himself how to execute the provisions of the law. If she had money she was made to pay a fine which the magistrates pocketed; if she had no money she might be sent to Bridewell, a House of Correction, where, should she be recalcitrant, she would be flogged every Sunday after morning service; or perhaps the magistrate might decide to order a public whipping in accordance with a sixteenth-century statue, not repealed until 1817, which provided that she "should be stripped naked from the middle upward and whipped till the body should be bloody."

It is not surprising that those poor pathetic girls who survived to practise their profession soon became as coarse as those who had driven them to it and in desperation and hunger used whatever means they could to excite the drunken passers-by and encourage them to come with them to a dark alley "by exposing their nakedness in the open street to all Passengers and using most abominable filthy expressions."

There was, however, nothing pathetic about the fat and jovial prostitute whom Jack first met that spring of 1723 at The Black Lion in Newton Street. Elizabeth Lyon, when Jack first knew her, was the wife or mistress of an infantry soldier who appears to have left her soon after Jack became so hopelessly infatuated with her. She was familiarly known to the customers of The Black Lion as "Edgworth Bess" and it seems likely that during the absences of her soldier she was employed there by the tavern-keeper, Joseph Hind, as one of his resident girls.

Joseph Hind was a former button-mould maker who had given up his trade for the doubtless more profitable one of inn-keeping and who had, Jack afterwards confessed, encouraged him in every form of vice and profligacy. He was one of the worst of publicans in an age when to be a publican at all in London was a tacit admission of corrupt if not of criminal tendencies. To promote their sales publicans encouraged the growing practice of paying wages on a Saturday night at the bar. The publican had an understanding with the employer, who arranged to pay out his men at, say six o'clock, but who did not in fact come with his money-bags until perhaps eleven o'clock or midnight, when the workers, egged on by the publican and his cronies, had spent all their expected wages on drink. The employer then gave most of the money to the publican after deducting his commission and the worker went back drunk and penniless to an anxious waiting wife and children. "Buying carcasses" was another common method by which the publican preyed upon the weakness of his customers. This entailed selecting a sufficiently weak-willed tradesman who could without too much trouble be encouraged to drink more than he could afford so that he got into debt. The publican then forced the tradesman to sign a promissory note which was then sold to someone else in the same trade, for whom the tradesman was accordingly obliged to work or go to prison as a common debtor.

Joseph Hind encouraged Jack's *affaire* with Edgworth Bess, for she was a heavy drinker and would make Jack spend money. Jack did so, but being a mere apprentice he had little to spend. He was determined to have more. It was not a big step in his present excited state of mind, intensely sexual and pleasure-loving as he now discovered himself to be, between the wanting money and the taking of it. He was just twenty-one and was suddenly enjoying life as he had never before expected to and was satisfying appetites which were delightful because he knew them to be wicked and which were the more intense because they were new. He was young for his years and always remained so. He was full of energy and enthusiasm and combined an almost studied wit with a very boyish charm. It was impossible not to like him and, as Edgworth Bess discovered as she grew to know him better, difficult not to love him. He was short but not uncommonly so in an age when men were generally shorter than they are today. He had a very pale skin and exceptionally large and attractive dark brown eyes; his mouth was full and humorous and sensual, and his small pear-shaped face with its wide brow and high cheekbones ended in a dimpled chin. His expression, sad and rather pathetic in repose, was often lightened by a quick disarming smile; his hands were large and strong and the fingers long and sensitive.

One day while he was engaged on some jobbing work at The Rummer, a famous bagnio at Charing Cross, he found himself in a room from which it would be the easiest thing in the world to steal two silver sppons. Without hesitation he picked them up and put them in his tool-bag. It was his first theft. He sold the spoons and spent the money on his mistress.

A few weeks later, out of funds again, he committed his second crime, but this time he was less successful. He was doing some repairs at the shop of Mr. Bains, a woollen broker in White Horse Yard, when a big roll of fustian caught his fancy. He thought that it would not be missed and that he would easily be able to get rid of it at a shilling a yard to his fellow apprentices in the neighbourhood. But once he had got it back to Wych Street he could not find anyone to buy it and taking it up to his attic room he hid it in his trunk. His fellow apprentice, an ineffectual and spiteful youth named Thomas, who had seen Jack offering it for sale, determined to find it and report the theft to his master Mr. Wood, who infuriated Thomas by seeming so fond of Jack in spite of his behaviour. When Jack was out one evening at The Black Lion Thomas rummaged through the few possessions in his trunk and eventually came across the fustian. Triumphantly he reported his find to Mr. Wood, who thought it his duty to apologize to Mr. Bains, regretting what had happened and promising to do what he could to make amends. Meanwhile Jack, who had heard of Thomas's betrayal, had come back to Wych Street unexpectedly, and so that Mrs. Wood should not know that he had been home he had broken into the house next door to the Woods' and climbed through an attic window of that house into his own garret to remove the stolen fustian. Afterwards, instead of returning the cloth as Mr. Wood asked him to, he went to Mr. Bains's shop and told the woollen broker that the stuff which had been found in his trunk had been bought for him by his mother from a weaver in Spitalfields. Mr. Bains then asked his mother to take him to the weaver, but after Bains and Mrs. Sheppard had spent a day together on an absurd wild-goose chase looking for this mythical weaver, Jack, unwilling to involve his mother any deeper in the business, sent most of the cloth back and there the matter might and should have rested.

But Jack by this time had developed a strong antipathy to the stern and pompous Bains and was determined to get his own back if he could. At the beginning of August he went by night from Wych Street to the shop in White Horse Yard, which by now he knew well, and carefully unscrewed the wooden bars at the cellar windows. Climbing steathily into the cellar and up the stairs into the shop he searched for something worth stealing and eventually came away with goods afterwards valued at fourteen pounds and seven pounds in cash. Quietly he screwed the wooden bars back over the cellar window and took his swag away to the lodgings of Poll Maggot, a prostitute whom he had met at The Black Lion and who was a friend of Edgworth Bess.

He now had enough money to do something which he had been intending to do for a long time: to escape from the servitude and boring monotony of his apprenticeship. He was an experienced joiner and expert locksmith and thought that he might well earn a good living on his own as a journeyman, instead of remaining for the next three years apprenticed to an unambitious jobbing carpenter who never undertook the construction of new buildings, which was the sort of work which Jack wanted to do and which might indeed have interested him enough to have kept him out of trouble. Furthermore he had on several occasions lately violently quarrelled with the Woods, who had warned him repeatedly against mixing with the customers of The Black Lion. Once after a morning's hard work at The Sun at Islington, hot and tired and no doubt remembering with irritation some disparaging remark of Wood's about his lover, he quarrelled with his master over the meagreness of the dinner provided for himself and his mate and losing his temper actually came to blows with him.

Some days later, hearing Mrs. Wood arguing with Edgworth Bess and her soldier in the courtyard outside the workshop, he picked up a stick and hurled it out of the window at the quarrelling group and, whether intentionally or not, hit Mrs. Wood in the face.

It was plain to the respectable and perhaps rather sanctimonious Woods that the unruly and ill-tempered apprentice was getting quite beyond them. They continued to treat him like a spoilt child while he was becoming a potentially dangerous man. They locked him out of the house at night only to find in the morning that he had without difficulty clambered up the wall and through his attic window. When they remonstrated with him about the debauched and dissolute company he kept, he flew into a furious temper. They worried about him because they loved him and because they felt responsible for him as they would have done for a son. But they did not know what to do with him.

It was Jack who decided the matter for them. Having deposited the money and the material he had stolen from Mr. Bains in Poll Maggot's room he came back to Wych Street only to get his things. He never slept in the Woods' house again.

CHAPTER FIVE

CRIME & PUNISHMENT

J ACK'S crime was a capital offence. He knew that if
he was caught and found guilty he would be hanged.
The thought seems to have worried him as little as
it worried most of his criminal contemporaries.
Hanging is even less a deterrent in an age of violence
than it is in an age of enlightenment and order. And in
1723 when violence was a part of the pattern of everyday
life and when over a hundred offences were punishable by
death hanging was not a deterrent at all.*

Not till many years later, when the first tentative
efforts were made to prevent crime by means other than
the ferocious punishment of offenders, did the crime wave
subside. For the moment the London streets remained
at night more dangerous than they had ever been before
or ever were again.

* A list of the capital statutes in force and created in the eighteenth
century is given in Volume I of Dr. Leon Radzinowicz's great work
A History of English Criminal Law (Macmillan, 1949).

Only the main streets and squares were dimly lit by flickering lamps burning uncertainly the cheapest whale oil. The back streets were not lit at all and even in the principal thoroughfares the lamplighters, who were notoriously ill-mannered and uncouth, were always willing to take a bribe from a footpad and promise that a lamp would burn out at a certain time.

An unprotected person walking along the streets at night ran the risk not only of being robbed but of being murdered or maimed as well. For the street robbers were a savage brutal lot and often "knocked people down and wounded them before they demanded their money." But these professional criminals were never so greatly feared as the young amateurs of the day, who roamed the streets with the express purpose of committing acts of barbarous cruelty against defenceless passers-by for the simple reason that they enjoyed it.

A number of these wild and drunken sadists grouped themselves together at the beginning of the century and formed a club later to be known and feared throughout London as "The Mohocks." Their name was derived from that of the most savage of Red Indian tribes and their only qualification for membership "was an outrageous ambition of doing all possible hurt to their fellow creatures." They were divided into different departments under an "Emperor." The most innocent department was known as "The Tumblers," who forced prostitutes and old women to stand on their heads in tar barrels and having grown tired of insulting them or pricking their legs with their swords, they sent the barrel rolling down-hill to end up for all they knew at the bottom of the river. "The Sweaters" and "The Dancing Masters" formed a circle round their victim and shouting insults at him made him jump up and down while they pushed their swords between his legs to keep him on the move, too drunk to know or care when they had cut through his ankles. Other departments specialized in facial disfigurement by flattening noses or boring out eyes. To work themselves up to the necessary pitch of enthusiasm for their ferocious games they first drank so much that they were quite "beyond the possibility of attending to any notions of reason or humanity."

In 1711 Swift was complaining that "it is not safe to be in the streets at night for them." He wrote in his *Journal to Stella* that "Lord Winchelsea told me today at Court that two of the Mohocks caught a maid of old Lady Winchelsea's at the door of their house in the park with a candle, and had just lighted out somebody. They cut all her face and beat her without provocation."

As they were a quasi-secret society their depredations were restricted to the hours of darkness, unlike those of The Bold Bucks, whose ravages were more particularly sexual and consequently, in an age when it was practically impossible to get a conviction for rape and when the age of consent was twelve, were more openly conducted. The members of The Bold Bucks, like most of those of The Mohocks, were of so-called gentle birth. The Duke of Wharton was one of the leading members, each of whom, before admittance to the club, had formally to deny the existence of God and to eat at a tavern every Sunday a formidable dish known as "Holy Ghost Pie."

While in the daytime The Mohocks slept or dawdled their time away in brothels or at the gambling table, the ordinary criminal was still on the look-out for suitable prey. A man who walked about without a sword or a stick was considered to be taking an unwarrantable risk, for "robbery was carried on to an extraordinary extent in the streets of London even by daylight." Doctor Johnson more than once was thankful that he knew how to defend himself and in 1720 ladies on their way to Court were armed with blunderbusses "to shoot at the rogues." The Duchess of Montrose was robbed by highwaymen one day as she was carried across Bond Street in her chair on her way back from Court and in 1726 the Earl of Harborough was stopped in his chair in Piccadilly in the middle of the morning.

These were not isolated instances. Twenty-five major robberies were reported in the streets of London in only three weeks in the winter of 1720. At Baretti's trial in 1769 several witnesses were called by the defence to swear that they had been subjected to ill-treatment and violent outrage in the neighbourhood of Haymarket. It was little wonder that Walpole wrote to a friend petulantly to complain that "one is forced to travel, even at noon, as if one was going into battle."

It had indeed by the middle of the century begun to resemble a war against society. The underworld was large and the criminal gangs strong and well organized. One of these gangs known as "The Thieves' Company" paid clerks to keep their books and to divide their profits, which amounted to about £500 a year for each member of the gang. Another gang was reported to have more than a hundred members who "have officers and a treasury and have reduced theft and robbery into a regular system."

The Resolution Club imposed on its members the strictest rules of professional etiquette. The principal rule was to "die mute," another "that whoever resisted or attempted to run away when stopped should be cut down and crippled." Those members of the public who prosecuted any member of the gang or who gave evidence against him should be marked down for vengeance. Forty toughs believed to be members of this gang attacked a watch-house in Moorfields where a fellow member was imprisoned. They rescued him, pulled the watch-house down, beat up the constable and robbed him. It is not surprising that the constables and magistrates and thief-takers of the time generally left these gangs alone.

"Officers of Justice," Fielding wrote in 1751, "have owned to me that they have passed by such criminals with warrants in their pockets against them without daring to apprehend them; and indeed they could not be blamed for not exposing themselves to sure destruction; for it is a melancholy truth that, at this very day, a rogue no sooner gives the alarm within certain purlieus than twenty or thirty well-armed villains are found ready to come to his assistance."

The extraordinary network of organized crime and vice in London revealed at the trial of Jonathan Wild in 1725 came as a surprise even to his contemporaries, who had learned to expect practically anything. Wild was accused not only of being a receiver and "confederate of criminals" and of forming a "corporation of thieves" but of dividing the whole country into districts and allocating to each a special gang; of appointing specialist gangs for church robbery and mobile gangs to follow the Court, the law circuits, and the various country fairs; of employing several artists and craftsmen to alter and reset jewellery and objects of art and of owning numerous warehouses where the enormous hoards of stolen property could be accommodated until they were sold to receivers in London or smuggled in his sloop to Holland.

Even when not a member of a gang there were still plenty of opportunities for the criminally inclined to make a dishonest penny. There was a wide variety of careers to choose from. Picking pockets seems to have been an overcrowded profession, but housebreaking provided a good living for many. There were numerous ways of making money by coney-catching, bat-fowling, or guinea dropping, and other variations of the confidence trick whereby the ingenuous countryman soon had his pockets emptied by the artful trickster with a plausible story to tell.

One of the most profitable of all crimes was coining and had been so for many years. As early as 1692 in that one year alone information was given of over three hundred coiners practising their craft in various parts of London. Coining and clipping coins were both treasonable offences and the punishment for treason was an agonizing death, but the profits were immense. John Moore, a tripeman executed at Tyburn for coining, had offered six thousand pounds for his pardon and his is not an exceptional case.

For those who were content with small takings for less dangerous work, there were jobs in and around the Fleet Prison, where clerical debtors, and those who looked as if they might be, carried on a business in quick marriages. A clergyman in the Fleet for debt was allowed to wander in restricted freedom "within the bounds of the Fleet," which stretched a mile in every direction. And within this area there were numerous signs depicting a male and female hand clasped together and beneath the picture the words: "Marriages performed within." Beneath the sign stood the renegade clergyman, "a squalid profligate fellow clad in a tattered plaid night gown with a fiery face and ready to couple you for a dram or a roll of tobacco." The more usual fee was a couple of guineas for a well-dressed couple, to three shillings or so for a couple that evidently could afford no more. If the couple had been brought in off the streets the pimp had his cut, and the tavern-keeper had his if the ceremony took place on his premises. The couple could have an important-looking document if the husband wanted it and all records of the marriage could be conveniently lost if a secret or bigamous marriage was required.

Hundreds of people lived entirely upon their earnings as pimps, procuresses, prostitutes' bullies, crimps, and male prostitutes. Hundreds more employed in taverns, prisons, brothels, and gambling houses earned a living which although perhaps not technically illegal was certainly not honest.

The *St. James's Evening Post* published a revealing "list of officers" whom any large gambling house might be expected to employ. There were "1. A Director who superintends the room. 2. An Operator who deals the cards at a cheating game called faro. 3. Two Crowpees who watch the cards and gather the money for the bank. 4. Two Puffs who have money given to them to decoy others to play. 5. A Clerk who is a check upon the puffs to see that they sink none of the money given them to play with. 6. A Sprit who is a puff of a lower rank, who serves at half salary while he is learning to deal. 7. A Flasher to swear how often the bank has been stripped. 8. A Dunner who goes about to recover money lost at play. 9. A Waiter to fill out wine, snuff candles, and attend in the gaming room. 10. An Attorney, a Newgate Solicitor. 11. A Captain who is to fight any gentleman who is peevish for losing his money. 12. An Usher, who lights gentlemen up and downstairs, and gives the word to the porter. 13. A Porter who is generally a soldier of the foot guards. 14. An Orderly Man who walks up and down the outside of the door, to give notice to the porter, and alarm the house at the approach of the constables; and 15. A Runner who is to get intelligence of the justices' meetings. Link boys, watchmen, chairmen, drawers... affidavit men, ruffians, bailees, *cum multis aliis.*"

Gambling was a profitable business. Enormous sums and even vast estates were lost and won in a single evening at loo or ombre or piquet. In one night Sir John Bland, who dissipated his great fortune playing hazard, "exceeded what was lost by the late Duke of Bedford, having at one period of the night (though he recovered the greatest part of it) lost two and thirty thousand pounds."*

Scores of rich men were ruined and formerly honest men turned to crime and "took," as they termed it, "to the road." Fielding, who was as likely as anyone to know, said that gaming was "the school in which most highwaymen of great eminence have been bred." The majority of highwaymen were impoverished gentlemen, former guards officers, or servants of gentlemen. They were sometimes high-spirited amateurs to whom highway

*The sums of money mentioned in this book may be multiplied by about five to give some idea of their present worth.

robbery appealed as a rather dangerous sport and whose
hero was Macheath, the amorous highwayman of *The
Beggar's Opera.* Brutal uncouth highwaymen such as
Dick Turpin were exceptions rather than the rule. They
were often indeed distinguished for their gallantry and
endeavoured to live up to their reputation as "Knights
of the Road," as they were romantically called. Reading
the reports of highway robbery in the newspapers of the
time, it is impossible not to be struck by their curious
quirks of behaviour. The celebrated Captain McClean
sent two letters of apology to a man whom he had
wounded accidentally when robbing him and offered to
give him back most of the valuables if he would meet him
at Tyburn Gate on a certain midnight. Another highwayman, having robbed the occupants of a coach at Maiden-
head Thicket, gave them back some of their money on
learning that they were on their long way to Bath. When
in 1751 the Shrewsbury coach was stopped by a single
highwayman "he behaved very civilly to the passengers,
told them that he was a stranger in distress, and hoped
that they would contribute to his assistance. On which
each passenger gave him something to the amount in the
whole of about 4*l.*, with which he was mightily well
satisfied, but returned some halfpence to one of them
saying he never took copper. He told them there were
two other collectors on the road, but he would see them
out of danger, which he accordingly did, and begged
that they would not at their next inn mention the robbery

nor appear against him if he should be taken up hereafter."
A particularly gallant robber on Wimbledon Common
after taking her purse from a young married lady
"politely demanded an elegant ring which he discovered
on her finger. This she peremptorily refused, saying,
'she would sooner part with life'; the hero of the turf
rejoined, 'Since you value the ring so much, madam,
allow me the honour of saluting the fair hand which
wears it, and I shall deem it a full equivalent!' The hand
was instantly stretched through the chariot window, and
the kiss being received, the highwayman thanked her for
her condescension, and instantly galloped off perfectly
satisfied with the commutation."

These stories, in the best romantic tradition of robbery
on the open road, are a welcome relief from the catalogue
of savage cruelties and senseless brutalities with which
most contemporary crimes were attended. But just as the
unimaginative rough-and-tumble ruffians of London were
undeterred by the furious punishments which were dealt
out to them, so these "collectors," as they euphemistically
called themselves, seemed undismayed by the putrefying
corpses of their comrades, dangling horribly in their
clanking and creaking chains, which from time to time
they were obliged to pass. An Irishman travelling in
England remarked on this. "Many gibbets are up all over
this common," he wrote, remembering a journey across
Finchley Common. "And I saw no less than five within a

pistol shot of each other, which made me wonder it did not deter these villains from such practices."

But it apparently did not deter them; rather did it alarm the innocent travellers who, driving towards the villages of Hampstead or Knightsbridge or across Hounslow Heath, could not fail to see these grisly reminders of the dangers of the road. There can, of course, be no doubt that the travellers were used to such sights. They could pass a corpse or a dismembered limb or the dead body of a baby with not much more distaste or pity than a sensitive person today feels on passing a butcher's shop where carcasses dangle on hooks. For the human body was not considered in any degree sacrosanct. The fallen heads of traitors were kicked unfeelingly into the gutter at Temple Bar and on more than one occasion the head of a murdered man was stuck up on a pole in a busy thoroughfare in the hope that a passer-by might be able to identify it. The head of the murdered Mr. Hayes was identified in this way. The story of his murder in 1726 is an interesting and by no means unusual example of the type of apparently motiveless and unfeeling murder which was not uncommon at the time.

Hayes was a hardworking and inoffensive little man whose shrewish and domineering wife made his life unbearable. She said to him once, so it was alleged at her trial, that she would think no more of killing him than to do away with a dog. She decided to prove her boast with the help of two lodgers in her house, Billings and Wood. Billings was thought by some to be Mrs. Hayes's lover, by others to be her illegitimate son. Whichever he was he seems to have had no hesitation in falling in with Mrs. Hayes's schemes. Wood needed more persuasion, but on being told that Hayes was an atheist and that on his death his wife would come into £1,500 which she would give to him, he offered no more resistance.

One evening after a lengthy drinking bout Hayes became so drunk that it was with difficulty that he stumbled upstairs and fell on his bed. As soon as he had passed out Billings came into the room with a hatchet and gave Hayes a fierce blow on the head with it, fracturing his skull, whereupon Wood believing him not to be quite dead delivered two more blows to finish him off. Mrs. Hayes, who had watched the performance, then directed the others to cut up the body to prevent identification. Wood obligingly cut off the head with his pocket knife and gave it to Mrs. Hayes, who said that she would take it away to boil it. The others disagreed with this and thought that it would be safer to throw the head into the river where it would be carried out to sea on the morning tide. So cutting up the rest of the body they put the bits into a box and wrapping up the box in an old blanket they threw it into a pond at Marylebone; the head they flung into the river at Westminster Horseferry.

The following day the head was seen floating near the bank of the river by a watchman who fished it out with his pole and handed it over to the parish officers. The head was washed and its hair was combed and it was stuck up on a pole in the churchyard of St. Margaret's, Westminster, where it was eventually recognized by both an organ grinder and a tailor. Mrs. Hayes was immediately questioned and giving evasive and contradictory excuses she was arrested. Billings and Wood, who were known to have been drinking with Hayes on the night of his murder, were also arrested, and Wood, on learning that the dismembered body had also been found, confessed his part in the crime. Billings shortly afterwards followed suit. But Catherine Hayes refused to admit that she had had any part in it. On being confronted in Bridewell with her husband's head which was pickled in spirit in a bottle, she rapturously took the bottle in her arms and weeping copiously, cried out: "It is my dear husband's head." The surgeon lifted the head out of the bottle so that she could inspect it more closely. She snatched it from him and kissed it passionately, asking if she might have a lock of its hair.

At the trial they were all three found guilty and sentenced to death. Wood died in prison before he could be executed, but Billings was hanged at Tyburn and his body was subsequently hung in chains beside the pool at Marylebone.

The fate of Catherine Hayes was not to be merely hanging, for she was guilty of petty treason, the crime of killing a person to whom was owed special allegiance.

The penalty of petty treason was burning and remained
so until 1789. Not, however, since the sentences of Judge
Jeffreys had been carried out following Monmouth's
Rebellion in 1685 had a woman been intentionally burned
alive, for it was customary for the hangman to mitigate
the sentence by strangling the woman as the faggots were
lit. In the case of the unfortunate Catherine Hayes the
hangman, who was believed to have been drunk, bungled
his job. As he tightened the rope round the woman's neck
the flames scorched his hand and he let go. Making no
further effort to help her, he and the spectators watched
her as she was slowly burned to death, frantically trying
to push the flaming sticks and brushwood away from her
and screaming in terror and pain.

Many of the hundreds of spectators who witnessed
this terrible punishment had travelled many miles to do
so. Punishments were always carried out in public so that
the people might be constantly aware of the wages of sin;
but the behaviour of the crowds on these occasions was
more appropriate to a cock fight than to the object lesson
in social morality which they were intended to provide.

Miscreants in the pillory always provided the public
with a good free show. The pillory was a large hinged
plank with three holes through which the victim was
obliged to put his head and his hands. It was erected on a
platform and was intended originally as a form of uncomfortable, but not necessarily painful, public disgrace.
It was far more than that.

Whenever it became known that a person was to be pilloried, a crowd collected in front of the platform armed with dead dogs and cats, buckets of excrement or rotting vegetation, stones and sticks, rotten eggs, and bottles. The hangman wasted no time on the platform, for as soon as he stepped up to it with his victims the shouting and pelting began. On occasions he was obliged to get up again to scrape the filth from the heads in the pillory because it was not unknown for a person to suffocate as the mud and rotten fruit splashed on his face and filled his nostrils and mouth.

The indignity of being covered with dung and mud by a laughing shouting mob was perhaps something from which it was possible soon to recover. But the possibility of losing his life in the pillory, and the probability of being seriously injured, were real dangers for which the victim must also have been prepared. A newspaper report describes the fate of two men pilloried on St. Margaret's Hill, Southwark. "One of them," the journalist wrote, "being of short stature and remarkably short necked, could not reach the hole made for the admission of the head. The officers of justice forced his head through the hole, and the poor wretch hung rather than walked as the pillory turned round. Previous to being put in he had deprecated the vengeance of the mob and begged for that mercy which in their exasperation at his crime, and their want of considering the consequences of their cruelty, they seemed very little inclined to bestow. He soon grew black in the face, and the blood issued from his nostrils, his eyes and his ears; the mob nevertheless attacked him with great fury. The officers, seeing his situation, opened the pillory, and the poor wretch fell down dead on the stand of the instrument. The other man was likewise so maimed and hurt by what was thrown at him that he lay there without hope of recovery."

These poor wretches were convicted of a homosexual offence which appeared always to enrage the mob to excesses of fury. In 1763 a homosexual was pelted to death in the pillory at Bow, and Ann Morrow, who had been found guilty of disguising herself as a man for the purpose of marrying three different women, was blinded by the stones flung at her by an exceptionally violent crowd. As might be expected, betrayers of the criminal class received similarly harsh treatment. In 1732 John Waller was pelted to death for perjuring himself in order to obtain the reward offered on the conviction of a highwayman.

An offence against authority, on the other hand, was of course in the eyes of the mob no offence at all. Daniel Defoe, who stood in the pillory for his pamphlet: *The Shortest Way with the Dissenters*, and the publisher who was pilloried for reprinting the famous No. 45 of *The North Briton*, were treated most respectfully, crowned with flowers and encouraged by cheers. Professional criminals were also usually treated with consideration, but in their case an appearance in the pillory was rare and was generally followed by some more savage punishment. In 1731 a forger, Japhet Crooke, after being in the pillory for an hour was "set on a chair on the Pillory, when the Hangman dressed like a butcher came to him, attended by two surgeons and with a Knife, made like a Gardener's Pruning Knife, cut off both his ears and with a Pair of Scissors slit both his nostrils which were afterwards seared with a Hot Iron."

The barbarity and severity of punishments was left very much to the discretion of individual magistrates and judges, who enforced the law according to the dictates of their own consciences and their knowledge of the criminal code. While hanging remained the legal punishment for so many trivial offences, from picking a pocket of more than a shilling to poaching a rabbit, the criminal law was bound to be open to intentional misinterpretation by sympathetic magistrates. And while it remained so complicated it is not surprising that justices were "as regardless of the law as ignorant of it."

Numerous strange anomalies in the criminal code were suffered to remain without question. Attempted murder, for instance, was merely a misdemeanour, while to snatch a watch out of a man's hand and run away with it was a capital offence. To steal fruit from a basket was a felony, but to gather fruit and then steal it was a trespass. On coming across these extraordinary inconsistencies one begins to have some sympathy with Fielding's Justice Thrasher, who, although expected to have at least a

nodding acquaintance with the hundreds of volumes in
which the ramifications of the law were contained, "never
read one syllable of the matter."

So long as the criminal law was so illogical and contradictory, there was some excuse for the haphazard and
unreasonable manner in which punishments were inflicted
for breaches of it. Bigamy seems to have been variously
punished by branding in the hand, transportation, or the
pillory. A burglar who had committed a capital offence
might get away with transportation. A prostitute might
be pilloried, whipped, or fined, or, if she was good-
looking and was brought before a magistrate such as the
lusty Colonel de Veil, she might be "examined privately"
in his "private closet for the examination of the fair sex"
and let off altogether.

Punishments also, of course, often depended to a large
extent upon the bribes that an offender could afford to
pay to avoid them. A magistrate just as any other official
concerned with the keeping of the peace turned an office
of honour into one of profit by means of the fines which
he imposed and pocketed and the bribes which he so
readily took. Charles Hitchen, the City Marshal, made a
practice of walking the streets at night "calling in at
several brandy shops and alehouses between [Temple
Bar] and Fleet ditch. Some of the masters of these houses
complimented the Marshal with punch, others with
brandy, and some presented him with fine ale, offering
their service to their worthy protector. The Marshal

made them little answer; but gave them to understand that all the service he expected from them was to give him information of pocket-books, or any goods stolen as 'a pay-back; for you women of the town' (addressing himself to the females of one shop), 'make it a common practice to resign things of this nature to the Bullies, and rogues of your retinues,—but this shall no longer be born with, I'll give you my word, both they and you shall be detected, unless you deliver all the pocket-books you meet with to me. What do you think I bought my place for, but to make the most of it? and you are to understand this is my man' (pointing to the Buckle-maker)*'to assist me. And if you at any time for the future refuse to yield up the watches and books you take, either to me, or to my servant, you may be assured of all being sent to Bridewell, and not one of you shall be permitted to walk the streets. For, notwithstanding I am under a suspension, (the chief reason of which is, for not suppressing the practices of such vermin as you) I have still a power of punishing, and you shall dearly pay for the least disobedience to what I have commanded.' ''

A magistrate then had far wider powers than he has today. He acted as a sort of Chief of Police, making and ordering arrests, sending prisoners up for trial and giving evidence for the prosecution. But he was not paid a salary, although Patrick Pringle has found evidence to suggest that Colonel de Veil, who began his magistracy in 1729,

*Jonathan Wild.

was secretly rewarded by the Government for his attempts to break up the big criminal gangs and to enforce the Gin Act and so became England's first paid magistrate.†† Colonel de Veil was of course an exceptional man. He was as corrupt as any other magistrate and he made, he said, £1,000 a year from fees and fines. But he was perhaps the only magistrate in London who made any attempt, even though he did so mainly for the wrong reasons, to enforce the law. As for the rest, they became magistrates solely and unashamedly for the money they hoped to make, and "would commit a servant to Bridewell at any time when a master or mistress desired it." It was with some justification that Walpole maintained that "the greatest criminals of this town are the officers of justice."

The enforcement of the law was made even more difficult by there being no police force. Even de Veil, who once said that he had brought to justice "above nineteen hundred of the greatest malefactors that ever appeared in England," had done so almost single-handed helped only by a few constables and thief-takers. It was not until Henry Fielding took over de Veil's appointment and his house in Bow Street that the first steps towards a paid police force were taken.

Fielding accepted his appointment in 1748, a year in which crimes of violence were becoming more alarmingly frequent than ever. He knew that if he were to fight this

†Patrick Pringle, *Hue and Cry* (Morrow, 1955).

crime wave with any hope of success he would have to rely on firmer support than he could expect from the doddering old watchmen and lazy corrupt constables into whose hands the safety of the public was entrusted.

He was in a few years' time to give in his novel *Amelia* his considered opinion of "the watchmen in our metropolis, who, being to guard our streets by night from thieves and robbers, an office which at least requires strength of body are chosen out of those poor old decrepit people who are from their want of bodily strength, rendered incapable of getting a livelihood by work. These men, armed only with a pole, which some of them are scarce able to lift, are to secure the persons and houses of his Majesty's subjects from the attacks of young, bold, stout, desperate and well armed villains.... If the poor fellows should run away from such enemies, no one I think can wonder, unless it be that they were able to make their escape."

These pathetic creatures were never paid more than a shilling a night and usually less. They were, although Fielding does not accuse them of this, as venal and inept as the constables and seem to have spent as much time in night cellars drinking gin as they did patrolling the streets. They were generally willing to look the other way for sixpence and if they were not it cannot have greatly mattered. During the wild and bloody Gordon riots in 1780 when Langdale's distillery in Holborn was burned down by the mob, liquor ran in rivers down the street and the people went crazy with delight and knelt down in the gutter to gulp down and choke upon the non-rectified spirits; while the flames leapt into the sky and the drunken mob ran yelling up and down the street, an observer standing by the wall of St. Andrew's church-yard noticed an old watchman passing by "with his lantern in his hand...calling the hour as if in a time of profound tranquillity."

Neither watchmen nor constables had any control whatsoever in times like these and might just as well have stayed at home. Constables, unlike watchmen, were not paid public servants. They were private citizens who were obliged by the State to take on the duties of a constable for a year at a time as a sort of spare-time job. Rather than perform the duties of a constable a man would delegate his unwanted authority to a deputy, paying the deputy a little—usually very little—for his trouble. There had soon developed, therefore, a small mercenary army of professional constables, corrupt and inefficient, who were avowedly in the racket for what they could get out of it. Being paid little by those whose proxies they were, they made up their incomes by accepting bribes and protection money.

Of the eighty constables who came under Henry Fielding's jurisdiction as Principal Magistrate of West-minster he found that he could trust only six. These six, trained by his assistant Saunders Welch, High Constable of Holborn, were essential to his plans for the Reform of

Law Enforcement. He fired them with his own enthusiasm and they, devoted to him, agreed to remain on as constables for another year as soon as he asked them to, although they could expect no payment other than the ordinary thief-taker's rewards. They became known ,and ultimately respected, as "Mr. Fielding's People" and they were the prototypes of the famous Bow Street Runners.

But during the first half of the century, while Mr. Fielding was still writing plays and as yet had no thought of reading for the Bar, it was necessary for the most part to rely for the apprehension of criminals upon the unreliable efforts of thief-takers, unpleasant and shifty creatures who slunk about the underworld watching and listening for information which might be of use to them.

The thief-taker was officially created towards the end of the seventeenth century by an Act which provided a reward of £40 for an informer on a conviction for highway robbery. Later Acts created rewards for most other offenders, from £40 for a housebreaker down to £1 for an army deserter. With the reward went a pardon, so that criminals should be further tempted to inform against each other.

As a thief-taker dared not interfere with a large and well-organized gang or a desperate criminal who might if acquitted seek him out and kill him, he concentrated upon first offenders and juvenile delinquents. A frequently practiced dodge was for two thief-takers to share the reward given on the conviction of a youth whom one of them had incited to commit some crime of which the other was a witness. In bad times it was always possible for a thief-taker to trump up a charge against a dense but innocent youth on a visit from the country.

Once committed to trial the innocent stood about the same chance of being acquitted as the guilty, which, to give the system its due, was quite a good chance.

Perjury was a full-time profession and perjured evidence could be given for the defence just as well as for the prosecution. "Straw men," as they were called from their habit of discreetly advertising themselves by sticking straw into their shoe buckles, walked up and down outside the Old Bailey or Westminster Hall until some lawyer offered them a tempting price for a useful few words in the witness box.

The juries were likely to be as biased as the witnesses were false. Special juries in the County of Middlesex, according to *The London Evening Post*, were "allowed an elegant dinner at Appleby's and five guineas a man if a verdict is given for the Government, otherwise they pay their own expenses."

But the bias of a jury, and of a judge for that matter, was just as likely to be in favour of the accused as against him. Rather than hang a woman for stealing a silver snuff box from a man's pocket the jury would value the box at elevenpence so that her crime became no longer a capital offence.

Even if condemned to death the accused might well be pardoned and be transported to the colonies in America instead of to Tyburn. In fact only about half the number of criminals who received the death penalty were executed.

So much depended upon the judge's interpretation of the law, his mood, his prejudices and sensibility, and upon the jury's opinion of the gravity of the particular crime of which the prisoner stood accused. There were precedents enough for juggling with the practice of the law if they felt inclined to do so and for making full use of the accepted double-thinking in applying it. But so long as the criminal laws remained so severe there were always judges and juries, magistrates, and justices who, prompted by fear or revenge, or a love of suffering, and sometimes a real belief in the necessity for suffering, were prepared to interpret these laws to the last letter of brutal severity. These were the men who sentenced the servant girl of fourteen to be burned to death for hiding her employer's whitewashed farthings and who sentenced to death by hanging a little boy of nine for stealing some goods from a shop window. And these were the men who sentenced to a ghastly death in the Press Room men who could not plead and, on one occasion, a man who, it was afterwards believed, was unable to plead because he was deaf and dumb. The object of submitting to this torture was that the estate of a man pressed to death could be willed to his chosen heirs, whereas if he were found guilty it would pass to the Crown.

The terrible words in which the threat of *peine forte et dure* was made were uttered according to a formula little altered since the early fifteenth century, when pressing to death took the place of starving to death as being considered more humane. Three times he was warned of the consequence of his obstinacy. If he continued obstinate, sentence was passed that "the prisoner shall be remanded to the place from whence he came, and put in some low dark room; he shall lie without any litter or anything under him, and that one arm shall be drawn to one quarter of the room with a cord, and the other to another, and that his feet shall be used in the same manner, and that as many weights shall be laid on him as he can bear and more. That he shall have three morsels of barley bread a day, and that he shall have the water next the prison, so that it be not current, and that he shall not eat the same day upon which he drinks, nor drink the same day upon which he eats; and he shall so continue till he die."

It was not an idle threat. But it rarely resulted in death for the prisoner. Rather than bear any longer the agony of breathing or the fear of the blood throbbing and surging in his ears bursting out of its veins, he asked for the favour of being taken back to the court to enter his plea.

His request was generally granted and a breach of the law was once more openly connived at. The weights were removed from the heavy board on his chest and the cords around his wrists and ankles untied. He was taken from the prison back to the courtroom. And there amidst the smells which he now no longer noticed and the indifference which was as frightening as the cruelty, the machinations and convolutions of his trial continued.

CHAPTER SIX

ALONE IN THE WORLD

═══

JACK'S first lodgings after leaving Wych Street seem to have been in the house of a Mr. Charles in Mayfair, where he was given the job of journeyman assistant to a carpenter whom Mr. Charles had employed to carry out some repairs.

The carpenter in view of Jack's extremely youthful appearance found it difficult to believe that the young man had served out his apprenticeship. But he was impressed by his skill and said nothing, thinking that he was lucky to have found so competent an assistant.

Jack, however, did not live up to his master's expectations, for on 23rd October he left the house with between seven and eight pounds' worth of silver spoons and four suits of clothes.

Some time later he got another job as journeyman assistant to a master carpenter in Fulham and while employed there he set up Edgworth Bess in lodgings in Parson's Green, spending as much time with her there as his new employment would allow.

One day when working at Fulham he met his brother Thomas, who was already a successful and well-established thief. After a few drinks together the two brothers confidently expected that working in partnership they would make their fortunes, as no house in London could be made safe from their combined depredations, from the determination and experience of the one brother and the daring skill of the other.

Their first joint enterprise was the theft of nearly sixty pounds' worth of goods from the shop of Mary Cook, a linen draper in Clare Street. Encouraged by their success they next broke into the house of a Mr. William Phillips in Drury Lane and once more got clean away, this time with a less valuable haul of goods belonging to Mrs. Kendrick, a lodger in the house.

This second burglary was the last one which they carried out together, for Thomas was caught red-handed as he tried to sell some of the stolen goods and was taken away to Newgate, where he turned King's evidence and impeached his brother and their accomplice Edgworth Bess.

Jack, warned in advance of his brother's treachery, immediately left his lodgings in Fulham and, collecting Edgworth Bess from Parson's Green before the peace officers arrived to pick her up, they went into hiding with friends at the Queen's Head alehouse in King Street, Westminster.

There was now a price of forty pounds on his head. He was a marked and wanted man. He began to wonder which of his criminal acquaintances and boozing companions would be the first to betray him. Forty pounds to them was a large sum of money and, as he was not a member of any gang and had no influential friends amongst the magistrates or in the underworld, a thief-taker would not be risking much in bringing him to justice.

After lying low with Bess in their room at the Queen's Head for a few days he began to grow restless. He persuaded himself that the first heat of the chase was cooling off and he could afford to take a few calculated chances. It was not, for instance, he considered, too great a risk to agree to meet James Sykes one evening at Mr. Redgate's victualling house to make up a foursome at skittles.

James Sykes, known to his intimates as "Hell-and-Fury," was a man he had met once or twice in the company of his friend Blueskin Blake. He was, Jack knew, a brutal and foul-tempered footpad, but as a friend of Blueskin he felt that he could trust him. Besides, it seemed, as he told Bess, an age since he had been out and he longed for a drink and a chat and a game of skittles.

When he arrived at Redgate's, Sykes greeted him in a friendly manner, bought him a drink, and introduced him to his companion. The fourth member of the party had not yet arrived, Sykes said, but would be along soon and so they began to play without him.

Skittles was a game at which Jack excelled and in his enjoyment at playing again he soon lost all thought of the danger he ran of being seen and recognized by someone who had no particular reason or wish to protect him. They had not been playing long when the fourth member of the party arrived. He was Mr. Price, a constable of the parish of Seven Dials. Sykes went forward to greet Mr. Price and led him towards his victim. Jack, intent upon his game, suspecting nothing, and with his back turned towards the newcomer, was introduced to him and immediately arrested.

He was taken before the nearest magistrate and committed for the night to St. Giles's Roundhouse.

The beadle in charge of the roundhouse already knew Jack well, as Edgworth Bess had been committed there the summer before on a charge of stealing a ring from a man whom she had accosted. On that occasion Jack, learning that his mistress was locked up inside, had banged furiously on the door until the beadle arrived. He demanded with indignation and anger that the innocent prostitute should be released. The beadle naturally refused the arrogant request and was about to shut the door when Jack jumped at him, wrenched the keys out of his hand and unlocked the door of the cell in which his lover was imprisoned. The beadle watched helplessly as the strong and wiry youth and powerful-looking woman walked imperiously out of his premises.

The beadle was determined that this disgraceful performance should not be repeated and this time locked Jack up in the strongest cell of the roundhouse on the top floor.

As soon as the beadle had left him Jack set his mind to work on the problem of how best to escape. The cell had a stout and impregnable door and the smallest of barred windows, too narrow for him to squeeze through. He could have broken the lock and pushed back the bolt of the door only with the help of tools which he did not possess. The only implement in his pocket was a razor.

The furniture of the cell consisted of a chair and a straw mattress. Standing on the chair he felt above him in the darkness and touched the ceiling. He decided to make a hole in the roof.

Having pulled the mattress close to the chair to catch the plaster and broken laths and so deaden the noise of their falling, he cut off the stretcher from the back of the chair and using his razor and the stretcher, he poked and scratched and cut away the laths and plaster until he came through to the tiles. While it had been easy to work so far in comparative silence there was no likelihood of his being able to remove the tiles with so little noise. If a tile became dislodged before he had a grip on it, it would slip down the sharp slope of the roof into the street below.

He worked quickly but cautiously and had loosened and carefully removed a number of tiles when his excitement at being so near the completion of his task made him clumsy. A tile slipped from his fingers and slithered down the roof. It fell on to the head of a man standing talking to a group of friends in the dimly-lit street below Jack's cell. They looked up quickly to see what else was likely to fall and as they did so Jack, realizing that there was no further need for caution, furiously hit at the tiles, scattering them in every direction until he had made a hole big enough to clamber through. He pulled himself up onto the roof, dragging his blankets up after him, and as the crowd gathered beneath him and the beadle rushed up the stairs and fumbled with the lock, Jack tied his blankets together and nimbly let himself down into St. Giles's churchyard. Jumping quickly from tombstone to tombstone and then over the churchyard wall he joined, in front of the roundhouse, the now enormous crowd which had collected quickly from nowhere as a London crowd seemed always able to do.

Pointing upwards several of the people in the crowd called to each other claiming that they could see the dark shape of the escaped prisoner as he clambered over the roof. Jack too pointed towards the roof and affecting great excitement shouted to his neighbour: "There he is, the devil. Behind that chimney stack." As every eye in the crowd turned towards the chimney stack Jack sauntered away and left them all wondering where he had got to.

He was at liberty for only a few weeks. On 19th May, strolling through Leicester Fields with a friend of his, a young footpad named Benson, he came across a man arguing with a prostitute. The prostitute had accosted the man and during the course of their discussion as to terms she had apparently picked his pocket of a gold watch. The man, having got the watch back from her, held it up in his hand in front of the girl's face as he angrily upbraided her. It was a chance too good to miss. Benson and Jack approached the angry couple and listened for a moment, as if out of idle curiosity, to the acrimonious discussion. Then taking advantage of an opportunity which momentarily presented itself Benson quickly stretched out his hand and snatched the watch from the man's grasp. He dashed away with it followed by Jack and escaped into the crowd.

Jack was not so lucky. Racing for all he was worth in the direction of Leicester House and hearing the shrill shouts of onlookers raising the alarm, he ran almost full tilt into the arms of a burly sergeant of the Guard who held him fast and handed him over to the constables. An hour or so later he was once again under lock and key.

His cell on this occasion was in St. Ann's Roundhouse

and the beadle, unaware of his growing reputation as a prison-breaker, unquestioningly admitted as a visitor the following morning the faithful Edgworth Bess. Tucked away amongst the provisions that his supposed wife brought the prisoner was the spike of a halberd. Making skilful use of this instrument it was the work of a minute or two to break open the door of his cell and get out into the corridor. Before he could get any farther, however, the beadle's wife saw him and shouted to her husband, who rushed up to prevent his escape. Taking no more chances with the slippery young customer the beadle took him down to the cellar and then secured him with manacles and fetters. Thinking, in view of her part in the attempted escape, he should keep the wife under surveillance too, he pushed Edgworth Bess into the cellar to keep Jack company and left them both there until it was time to bring them up before the magistrate.

Mr. Justice Walters, when he saw the young couple, told them that if they would give him some information which led to the arrest of any of Jack's associates or accomplices he would deal very lightly with him. Jack affecting an honest and zealous desire to be of assistance to the magistrate in the prosecution of his duty said that he would be pleased to give him what help he could and promised to impeach his friends in accordance with the magistrate's wishes. When it came to the point, however, the information which Jack gave him was so useless and misleading that Mr. Walters committed them without

further discussion to the New Prison, Clerkenwell, telling
them that if they decided to give any proper information
there was still time for them to do so, but if they persisted
in their unwillingness to help he would have them
committed to the less pleasant prison at Newgate.

Described on the notice of commitment as man and
wife they were permitted to share the same cell at the
New Prison, where the governor, Captain Geary, warned
of Jack's past record, put them both in the Newgate
Ward, the strongest in the whole prison. Determined
that Sheppard should not make a fool of him, as he had
done the beadle at St. Giles's, he made the chances of his
escape even more remote by impeding his movements
with a pair of weights and a heavy chain. He also, contrary
to the usual custom, forbade his turnkeys to allow the
prisoner any visitors. But several of his friends nevertheless bribed their way into his ward and slipped him
various files and saws and other tools which he would
find useful in making his escape.

By the evening of Sunday, 24th May, he had all the
implements and tools he needed and he set to work. First
he filed through his fetters and then having more freedom
of movement he turned his attention towards the window
of his cell.

The window was small, but he thought that even the
corpulent Bess could just squeeze through it if he could
file through the iron bar and the wooden beam which
protected it. Helped by Bess he soon filed through the

bar, but the beam was a more formidable obstacle. It was quite nine inches thick and to file through it at each end with his file would take hours. Fortunately amongst the collection of tools with which his friends had provided him was a gimlet. Using this with practised skill he bored numerous holes through the beam at each end, until it was so weakened that he was able to knock it out.

Jack looked out of the window and saw that the yard beneath was at least twenty-five feet below him, so that even by tying their blankets together the rope which they might thus make would still not be long enough to reach the ground. He told Bess to take off her skirts and petticoats and tying them to the blankets he fixed one end of his now adequate rope to the end of the iron bar and threw the other end out of the window. In a minute he and Bess had slipped down the makeshift rope to the yard.

They had escaped from the prison, but they were now in another one. For where the walls of Clerkenwell New Prison ended the precincts of Clerkenwell Bridewell began and in front of them across the bare yard of Bridewell was the high wall of this other prison, standing between them and their freedom, twenty-two feet tall and topped by a row of sharp and menacing iron spikes.

Jack crept stealthily along the wall in the darkness trying to find a way of getting through into the street. But the only alternative to making an attempt to scale the wall was to try and climb over the enormous wooden

gates which, as he had discovered on his silent recon-
naissance, were unguarded.

The gate seemed a less formidable obstacle than the
wall, so tying the end of his home-made rope round his
waist he began his attempt to reach the top of it. The first
few feet of the climb were not too difficult, as clutching
hard onto the iron studs with the tips of his strong fingers
he found footholds on the bolts and lock boxes. But even
when he was standing on the highest bolt, the surface of
the gate, its flatness broken only by the rows of thick
studs, still stretched high above him towards the dark
sky. Balancing with extraordinary agility on his precarious and slight foothold, he took the gimlet from his
pocket and using it with speed and dexterity and at the
same time maintaining his delicate balance he made two
more holes for his feet in the wooden surface above his
head. Once more gripping the studs between his powerful
finger-tips he pulled himself up until he could make use
of the footholds which he had made.

Patiently he began the work again. This time his
foothold was firmer and he had more freedom of movement in which to work without danger of losing his
balance.

When he had made his new footholds and had clambered up to make use of them he could just reach the top
of the gate. Closing his fingers round the thick curved
piece of wood he pulled himself up into a sitting position
astride the gate and called softly down to Bess to hold

onto the end of the rope of blankets. Uncertainly balanced and tired out after his previous exertions he could scarcely, pulling as hard as he could, lift the plump and heavy girl off the ground, but by making a last and furious effort he tugged her up and let her down into the street on the far side of the gate. Then, screwing the gimlet into the wood, he tied the end of the rope round it and climbed down himself to join Bess outside the prison walls.

Not long after this remarkable escape Jack committed the most successful burglary of his career. He was lucky in his choice of a victim, but less so in his choice of an accomplice.

He had met Anthony Lamb some weeks previously in The Black Lion. Lamb was the nephew and apprentice of a Mr. Carter, a mathematical-instrument maker whose workshop was not far from Mr. Wood's in Wych Street. He had told Sheppard of a master tailor named Barton who had lodgings in the Carter household and who in Lamb's opinion was a rich man. He promised to leave the street door open any night Jack cared to call on Mr. Barton. When Jack did call he came with a friend, a tough cooper named Grace who crept up to Barton's room to hold a pistol to his head should he wake. But Jack had chosen his night well. The tailor had been to a party and snored drunkenly while Jack ransacked his possessions and took away his best suits together with various articles, banknotes, and cash to the value of nearly three hundred pounds.

Early the following morning a neighbour noticed that the door of the Carter house was open and came over to investigate. He found the house topsy-turvy and the tailor still sleeping heavily. The young apprentice was immediately suspected, as he was well known as a dissolute youth who spent more time than he should drinking with the unsavoury customers of The Black Lion, and after being threatened and dragged out of bed by his hair he confessed to his small part in the crime. He also admitted that Jack Sheppard and the cooper Grace were involved, but insisted, no doubt with truth, that he did not know where they could be found. And by the time the stolen goods were advertised they had already been sold to a fence at an alehouse in Lewkenors Lane.

The weak and indeterminate young apprentice was, however, some help to the authorities and indirectly brought about Jack's recapture. For he confessed in his sudden fright and humiliation to a great deal more than he need have done, and in hoping to escape punishment himself heaped accusations upon his companions. He said, for instance, that Sheppard's next burglary was to be at the house of his former master and benefactor William Kneebone, and when on the night of 12th July Kneebone was, in fact, robbed of goods to the value of about fifty pounds Sheppard was immediately and justly suspected.

The details of this burglary are, to say the least, obscure. Jack vehemently maintained at his trial that William Field, the chief prosecution witness, was lying when he testified that he had taken a leading part in the robbery. Jack swore that this was not so and that Field, whom *The Daily Journal* described as a "noted Witness," had never been there at all. Field's story was that at midnight on 12th July Sheppard accompanied by himself and Blueskin Blake had broken into Kneebone's cellar in Little Drury Lane by cutting through two oak beams which had been weakened by occasional sawings at intervals during the previous fortnight. From the cellar they had crept up into the shop and had spent three hours rummaging amongst the rolls of linen and cloth and ransacking the drawers and cupboards while the Kneebone family slept peacefully upstairs.

Jack constantly asserted that whilst it was true that Blueskin and he had robbed Kneebone, Field had learned the details of the robbery not from experience but from what he had overheard afterwards and that the cloth which the "damned perjurer" produced at the trial, was in fact stolen by him from the stables at Westminster Horseferry which Jack had rented as a depository for stolen goods.

It seems likely that this was so and that Field had perjured himself as Jack so passionately insisted. For Field lodged with Blueskin's mother, who kept a brandy shop in Rosemary Lane, and could have discovered easily enough from the garrulous Blake how the burglary was effected without actually having taken part in it. Furthermore there is no evidence that Field was ever arrested for his part in the crime or that he was obliged to turn King's evidence in exchange for his pardon. He seems to have come forward willingly as a prosecution witness.

There is some evidence, on the other hand, that Field was in the pay of Jonathan Wild and this suggestion alone is enough to throw real doubt on the just conduct of the trial.

Several days after the robbery when the chances of either apprehending the criminals or recovering the stolen goods seemed to be quickly growing more and more slender, Kneebone approached Wild. And Wild set to work with a will. The first indication that Wild was interested in the Kneebone robbery was given on 17th July, when his name appeared in an advertisement in *The Daily Post* offering twenty pounds and a pardon to anyone who would "voluntarily surrender himself and discover his A complices in the robbery of one Piece of Scarlet Drab Cloth with several pieces and Remnants of colour'd Broad Cloth, 2 silver Spoons, a light tye Wigg and other Things from Mr. Wm. Kneebone Woollen Draper at the Angel the Corner of Drury Lane in the Strand."

For some time now the self-styled "Thief-taker General" had been angered by the reputation which Sheppard

Jack Sheppard escaping with Edgworth Bess from the New Prison, Clerkenwell, May 1724

from an illustration by George Cruikshank to *Jack Sheppard* by W. Harrison Ainsworth, 1839

Jack Sheppard escaping from St. Giles's Roundhouse, April 1724

from an illustration by Jack Sketch in *The History of Jack Sheppard*, 1839

Jack Sheppard, helped by Edgworth Bess and Poll Maggot,
escaping from the Condemned Hold in Newgate,
31st August 1724

from a contemporary print

had built up for himself as a housebreaker and criminal hero. Wild considered himself, with some justification, the ruler of the underworld; and a thief who made a living and a name for himself outside his organization was a danger to its successful running. If Wild's organization was to flourish ideally every accomplished professional thief in London must belong to it. There must be no colourful outsiders to demonstrate that it was possible to manage on one's own. Jack was too much of an individualist to get on with Wild. He had been, he afterwards confessed, to one of Wild's levees, but "caring not for his acquaintance" they never had "any dealings together."

Wild had then an urgent and personal reason for wanting to help Mr. Kneebone apart from any reward that he might earn by doing so.

Jack had unwittingly made in the Thief-taker General a relentless and a very dangerous enemy.

CHAPTER SEVEN

JONATHAN WILD

—

JONATHAN WILD'S father like Jack Sheppard's was a carpenter and it was into a poor but honest family like Sheppard's that Wild had been born in Wolverhampton in 1683. He was apprenticed when he was fifteen to a buckle maker in Birmingham and while he was still in his apprenticeship he married and had a son. Soon growing tired of marriage and buckle making, however, he deserted his family and set off for London. As he had no money he obtained a free lift in a carriage by exciting the pity of a lady traveller by means of a peculiar ability he had for dislocating his hip at will and appearing therefore to be painfully lame.

Not many months after arriving in London he got badly into debt and landed up in the Wood Street Compter, which was at that time one of the worst of the London prisons. Being unable to pay for the privilege of having a bed, which would have cost one and threepence a week, he was at first put into a ward known as the Hold which had a succession of shelves arranged around the walls in tiers to serve as bunks and which was used by its occupants not only as a dormitory but as a dining-room and kitchen as well, and indeed by most of them as a latrine. In order to escape from this terrible stinking place and to improve his diet, which in default of charity comprised no more than the regulation stale loaf and water, he undertook all manner of menial tasks and errands for the turnkeys and officers of the prison and for the wealthier prisoners who could afford to live in less loathsome parts of the building.

While he was engaged in thus improving his lot he met a prostitute named Mary Milliner who, having an extensive acquaintance amongst the criminal class, and an immense knowledge of criminal activities, taught him all she knew of the underworld outside the prison walls.

By the time he had made enough money in prison to pay his debts, Mary Milliner was not only his mentor but also his mistress, and the couple decided on being released from the Compter to go into partnership.

"The first business they went upon together was that of the buttock and twang or in other words the whore's bully." They found this business sufficiently profitable for them to settle down to a quieter life by opening a brothel in Lewkenors Lane. A few months later they moved to another house in a more lucrative neighbourhood, in Cock Alley opposite Cripplegate Church. Both these establishments were not only brothels which catered mainly for the criminal class, they were also receiving houses for stolen goods. Mr. and Mrs. Wild were thus giving their public two services at once and were allowing the robbers of the district, as one of their customers once put it, to kill two birds with one stone.

Mary Milliner's wide circle of friends and acquaintances amongst the burglars of the town and her intimate knowledge of their tricks and secrets made her the ideal partner in a business undertaking of this nature, but Wild knew only too well that although receiving was a profitable occupation it was a very dangerous one too. A law had recently been passed making the receiving of goods, knowing them to be stolen, a felonious practice and there was only one punishment for a felony.

This law had hit the robbers hard, for knowing that to be caught dealing in stolen goods was punishable by hanging the receivers made sure that the risks they ran were well worth while. By the time the receiver had satisfied himself that his profit justified his risk there was little enough in it for the thief. Jack Sheppard himself knew this as well as anyone. "I declare," he confided to Defoe, "that when goods the intrinsic value whereof has been £50 have been in my hands I have never made more than £10 of them clear money; such a discount and disadvantage attends always the sale of such unlawful acquirements."

Wild, having conceived a plan for the evasion of the law and for the profit of both himself and the thieves, sent out an invitation through the underworld's grapevine to

every successful professional burglar in London to attend
a meeting at his house. When the motley, dishevelled,
and rowdy assembly had quietened down Wild addressed
them in the half-threatening, half-bantering tones which
were already becoming familiar to his listeners. This, it
has been suggested by a contemporary, is the canting
speech he made to them:

"You know, my bloods, that as trade goes at present
you stand but a queer chance for when you have made
anything if you carry it to the fencing culls and flash pawn
brokers, those unconscionable dealers in contraband
goods will hardly tip you a quarter of what it is worth;
and if you offer it to a stranger it's ten to one but you are
babbled. So that there is no such thing as a man living by
his labour; for if he don't like to be half starved, he must
run the hazard of being scragged, which let me tell you
is a damned hard case. Now if you'll take my advice I'll
engage to pay back the goods to the cull that owns them
and raise you more cole upon that account than you can
expect from the rascally fencers; and at the same time
take care that ye shall be all bowmen."

The idea was not original, but Wild made it work. A
thief when he had committed a burglary told Wild whom
his victim had been and gave him a list of what he had
stolen from him and where the goods were now kept.
Wild then went to the house which had been broken into
and introduced himself to the owners.

"I happen to know," he would say to them, "that you
have been lately robbed and a friend of mine an honest

broker having stopped a parcel of goods upon suspicion, I thought I could do no less than give you notice of it as not knowing but that some of them might be yours; if it proves so (as I hope it may) you may have them again provided that nobody is brought into trouble and the broker has something in consideration of his care."

The arrangement usually proved satisfactory to all parties and Wild, who, as it appeared, accepted nothing directly from those who had been robbed but got his cut from the mythical broker, infringed no existing law. The business became so profitable and Wild became so well known that instead of calling on those who had been robbed he opened an office in his house in Cock Alley where the victims might call on him.

Wild was, so it seemed, a sort of Lost Property Consultant. He had in his office a clerk who entered the particulars of what his clients had lost in an imposing-looking volume and who charged them each a fee of five shillings for the benefit of his master's advice. Wild checked through the particulars in his clerk's book with the list which the robber had given him, noting carefully any discrepancies between the two lists and thus keeping a watch on any burglars who were foolhardy enough to keep back from him anything which they thought they might sell better elsewhere.

The client was asked to be good enough to call back within a day or so when news might be received of his stolen valuables. On his return he was greeted warmly and respectfully. "Why indeed, sir," Wild might tell him, "I have heard something of your goods but the person I sent to inquire tells me that the rogues pretend that they can pawn them for more than you offer and therefore if ever they make restitution it must be upon better terms. However if I can but once come to the speech of the rascals I don't question that I shall bring them to reason."

If, as often happened, his client immediately suggested increasing his offer Wild would as likely as not, with a convincing parade of honest concern, advise against such a course. When, therefore, the goods were eventually recovered for less cost than their rightful owners would have been prepared to pay, Wild was thanked with compliments as to his honesty, which advanced both his reputation and his business.

If his stock stood high with the honest public it stood even higher with the thieves. For not only was burglary once more a profitable occupation but small things, such as notebooks, letters, miniatures, receipts, sentimental trinkets, and all manner of items which could easily be carried in the pockets, were now of great value and could be sold to Mr. Wild.

The number of robberies increased to such an extent that Parliament in 1718 passed a new Act which made it a felony to take a reward under the pretence of restoring stolen goods without prosecuting the thieves who stole them.

The Act was directed personally at Jonathan Wild.

But after he had made a few alterations in the technique of his business he carried on as before, not so surely evading the law but certainly avoiding any prosecutions for flagrant breaches of it. His office had to be closed, but now his contact with his clients—who often had as little inclination to go to the trouble and expense of prosecuting the thieves as he had—was carried on by intermediaries in the streets and coffee houses. Sometimes Wild would suggest that the victim should advertise his loss in the newspapers and offer a satisfying reward to anyone who should find and bring the stolen goods to him "and no questions asked."* When Wild was asked what he wanted out of it he would say piously that he was activated only by an honest desire to do good and if he was given anything it could only possibly be out of generosity and was not to be considered a reward but a favour. It seemed coincidentally that if Wild was granted such a favour the goods were returned.

Whenever it was difficult to do business with a client Wild did not disappoint the thief by refusing to take the stolen goods off his hands. He had the goods stored in

*These advertisements appeared regularly in the newspapers of the time. The following, which is typical of hundreds, was inserted by one of Wild's clients in *The Daily Courant* on October 26th, 1723: "Lost out of an apothecary's shop near the Hermitage Bridge on Tuesday night a Brass Mortar weighing about 90 pounds. Whoever brings it to Mr. Adamson near the Hermitage-Bridge or to Jonathan Wild in the Old-Bailey, shall have 30s Reward and no Questions ask'd: If offered to be pawned or sold pray stop it, or if already pawned or sold your money again."

his warehouse until he had collected enough swag from other thieves to make up a cargo for the sloop he had bought for carrying off such surplus goods to Holland and Belgium.

And so it was that his receiving business flourished and he became a wealthy and indeed a celebrated man. His successful dealings with the gentry and the nobility and the dignitaries of the Church gave him ideas and ambitions not in keeping with his establishment in Cock Alley or with the whore who lived there as his wife. One day after a fierce argument with the woman he swore that "he would mark her for a bitch" and cut off one of her ears with the sword which he had taken to wearing. He took another and better-class mistress and moved to a smarter house in Old Bailey.

He was, he felt, going up in the world as a person of his consequence should. He walked the streets now dressed as a gentleman and carrying a sword. He even put himself forward as a candidate for public office under the Crown, and submitted a petition to the authorities in which he listed his rightful claims to the gratitude of the public and said boldly that he was "very desirous of becoming a freeman of this honourable city." On occasions he could be seen marching about with a silver staff in order to impress the populace with the fear of his supposed authority. He knew how effective the appearance of authority could be in the successful pursuit of criminal activities, for he had some time previously been the unofficial assistant of Charles Hitchen, the City Marshal, an officer of the law whose large income was principally derived from the bribes and protection money he accepted from those who feared his power and authority to bring them to justice and his confessed willingness to perjure himself whenever it might be profitable for him to do so.

An interesting example of the activities of the City Marshal was provided by Wild himself, who, in his reply to Charles Hitchen's *The Regulator*, shamelessly caused to be published various stories of their adventures together.

One night [Wild's ghost writer begins one of his numerous stories of Hitchen's abuse of his authority] the Marshal and Buckle-maker being abroad in their walks, not far from the Temple, they discovered a Clergyman pissing against the wall, in an alley to which he had retired for modesty-sake. Immediately a woman of the town, lying in wait for prey, brushed by the Clergyman, he saying aloud,'What does, what does the woman want?' The Marshal instantly rushed in upon them, seizing the Clergyman, bidding his man secure the woman. The Clergyman resisted, protesting his innocence (which his language to the woman confirmed) but finding it to no purpose, he desired he might be permitted to go into an Ironmonger's house near; but the Marshal refused, and dragged him to Salisbury-court end, where he raised a mob about him; and two or three gentlemen that knew the parson happened to come by, asked the mob what they were doing with him, telling them he was chaplain to a noble lord. The rough gentry answered,'Dam him, we believe he is chaplain to the devil, for we caught him with a whore.' Upon this the gentlemen desired the Marshal to go to a tavern, that they might talk with him without noise and tumult, which he consented to. When they came into the tavern, the Clergyman asked the Marshal by what authority he thus abused him? The Marshal replied, he was a City-officer (pulling out his staff) and would have him to the Compter, unless he gave him very good security for his appearance the next morning, when he would swear he caught him with the whore, and his hands under her petticoats. The parson seeing him so bent upon perjury, which would very much expose him, sent for other persons to vindicate his reputation, who, putting a glittering security into the Marshal's hand (which they found was the only way to deal with such a monster in iniquity) the clergyman was permitted to go off.

Wild's association with Hitchen was short-lived. Having learned the tricks of the trade he quarrelled with the City Marshal, who had in any event now been dismissed from his office, and broke off relations with him. Armed with his silver staff, his sole pretence to proper authority, he set up on his own.

His activities as an irregular and unauthorized trading Justice, however, occupied only a small part of his time. So for that matter did his receiving business which, managed by his intelligent and trustworthy clerk, was after a few years a sideline which practically ran itself. From 1718 onwards he concentrated on his principal and chosen work, that of organizing the ragged heterogeneous drifting and generally stupid criminal class into a strong and well-disciplined underworld working for his personal profit.

He worked hard and purposefully and by the early 1720's, in so far as crime was organized at all, he was its organizer. There had, of course, always been criminal gangs in London ever since London had become a town, but these gangs had never before considered the possibility of joining forces in the profitable predatory war against society which Wild envisaged. It was Wild's intention that each gang should be specially trained in a particular form of crime and have its recognized zones of activity and its accredited leader. Wild himself did not want to lead any gang; he wanted to advise them all, to give them ideas and suggestions, to put them up to schemes and dodges and rackets which they could not have thought of themselves. Ideally each parish would have two or three gangs specializing in street robberies or housebreaking, others specializing in confidence tricks or blackmail, others attending to the exploitation of vice, the collection of protection money from shops and brothels, coining, or murder.

How near Wild came to his ideal it is impossible now to say. It certainly does seem, however, that by 1725, when his career came to its abrupt close, he had had more than a little success. There were, of course, individualists who refused to conform, particularly amongst the highwaymen, who were notoriously independent, and there were other criminals over whom, and criminal activities over which it was impossible to impose any form of authority. Nevertheless since Wild's grip on the underworld relaxed no one has ever held the same position as he did and many have tried.

He maintained his unique and profitable place in the

hierarchy of the criminal class by a strange mixture of abilities and vices, by calculating shrewdness, and complete insensitivity.

He had a reputation for keeping his word. No criminal sent for by Wild and promised a safe conduct had reason to fear that the promise would be broken. If the interview was successful and the criminal agreed to Wild's suggestion all was well, but if he did not, Wild sent him away with the threat that although he would be allowed this time to go away in safety as he had been promised, if he saw Wild again he "would see an enemy."

It was far from an idle threat. Wild had as good a memory for a face as he had for a fact, and as an aid to his memory he kept a big notebook with dates and figures, details, names, and memoranda which would help him in securing the prosecution of most of the criminals in London. It was in his power, he once boasted, to hang every thief in the metropolis. If the evidence was not all it might be, he would buy more, and if the new perjured evidence was insufficient, he would buy the judge and jury too. But just as he was an implacable enemy to those who had defied him or stood in his way he was a loyal friend to those who were loyal to him. He secured an acquittal as effectively as he arranged a conviction. No one who worked obediently for Wild had need to fear a ride to Tyburn. Prosecution witnesses were bribed or mysteriously disappeared on the day of the trial, defence witnesses with faces "shining with honesty" and an apparent desire to please ingratiated themselves with a jury whose members had already been biased by a good meal and the promise of better things to follow. And there was always "Mr. Wild's book," full of valuable and carefully tabulated secrets which could be brought out to secure the conviction of an enemy in exchange for the acquittal of a friend. For justice was a bazaar and one criminal could, with far more ease then than now, earn his own release by informing against another. Law and order could after all, in a rough and tumble town without police, be maintained only by means of a system of barter. The conviction of one criminal was as good as the conviction of another, and if the acquittal of one offender was the only price to pay for the execution of two others, it was not a bad bargain at that. And so Mr. Wild's book was as highly thought of by his loyal followers as it was feared by those outside his protection and beyond the narrow limits of his friendship.

And that part of the underworld beyond the patronage of Jonathan Wild was a dangerous place to live and to carry on business. Wild believed strongly that anyone not for him was against him and was therefore fair game for him in his quasi-respectable role as "Thief-taker General."

His fame and success as a thief-taker not only kept his enemies in fear of him and his own men respectful, but also gave him a reputation amongst the general honest public as a useful and relentless pursuer of hardened criminals. He had no doubt that such a reputation would help him in his receiving business and would at the same time set him on his way to that advancement in public life which seemed to him so desirable. He was careful to ensure that his activities were given full publicity and few weeks passed without a notice of a new arrest appearing in the Press. Some reports are more sensational than others, and one such report indicating the dangers involved in operating outside Wild's empire appeared in the spring of 1724 in a newspaper which recorded that Wild had been successful in apprehending a gang of about a hundred street robbers, in Southwark, and had been instrumental in getting most of them committed to prison. Thief-taking on that scale was a very profitable business apart from those other considerations which first induced Wild to take it up. It was also for a man of Wild's temperament a congenial occupation. No one knew better than he how to handle a man hunt and no one enjoyed one more. His methods are effectively illustrated by his determined pursuit of the murderers of Mrs. Knap.

Mrs. Knap was murdered one night in 1716 by five footpads as she walked home with her son from Sadler's Wells.

A large reward was offered for discovering the villains. Jonathan immediately made it his business to find out the murderers. By the description given of some of them, he knew the whole gang; and, with the assistance of his man Abraham, took three of them, who were tried, and afterwards hanged for the same. But Timothy Dun (one of the gang) was not yet taken, for he had removed his lodgings, and kept himself so close, that not a word was to be heard of him at any of the cases.* But this did not discourage Jonathan; he knew that the fellow could not live long in such a private manner, for he must either follow the old business, or starve; and offered to lay a wager of ten guineas that he would have him before the next sessions; some of his acquaintance accepted the offer, and the money was deposited.

Dun, grown weary of his confinement, and willing to know if Wild was still in quest of him, sent his wife to get what intelligence she could. She went to Mrs. Seagoe's where Jonathan lodged, and staid there all the afternoon. When she went away in the evening, Wild sent a man after her to dog her home. She took water at Blackfriars, and crossed to the Faulcon. He followed in another boat. She suspecting him, crossed again to White-friars. He was presently after her, and she, perceiving it, took another boat to Lambeth. He followed her, but it being now dark, and he keeping at a convenient distance, she thought she had lost him, and so went directly to her lodgings in Maid-lane, near the Bankside, in Southwark. But he watched her so narrowly, that he saw where she went in, and, that he might not mistake the house the next day, he marked the door with a piece of chalk, and then returned with the news of his success.

Early in the morning, Wild, his man Abraham, Riddlesden and Horney, and another, went to Dun's lodging, which was up two pairs of stairs. He, hearing them at the door, got out of his back window upon the roof of a pantry, the lower part of which was not above seven or eight feet from the ground. Abraham getting into the back yard, and seeing Dun upon the

*See Glossary.

tiles, fired a pistol and wounded him in the shoulder, so that he rolled down into the yard, and then, though there was no fear of his escaping, Riddlesden shot him in the face with small shot.—Thus Jonathan won the ten guineas and Timothy was hanged.*

Wild's house in Old Bailey was chosen principally for its closeness to the court so that he had only a short way to go when he had to make his frequent appearances as chief prosecution witness. He lived here in comfort solaced by a succession of mistresses and guarded by a number of trusted servants most of whom had illegally returned from transportation and consequently knew that it was in their master's power to turn them over to the authorities at the first sign of disobedience.

He walked about in the town, closely watched by his bodyguard, alert and careful, caring nothing for the hatred which surrounded him, and miraculously escaping year after year the vengeance of his numerous enemies who reviled him with savage anger and wished him dead. He was cursed with fury, attacked often, wounded and scarred, but somehow he stayed alive.

He narrowly escaped death in October 1724 in the courtyard of the Old Bailey Sessions House while waiting to give evidence at the trial of Jack Sheppard's friend and accomplice Blueskin Blake. Noticing the forlorn Blueskin

---

*"An answer to a libel, entitled A Discovery of the conduct of receivers and thief-takers in London... written by C———s H———n wherein is prov'd who is originally the Grand Thief-Taker, etc." (1718).

standing disconsolately in the courtyard, Wild went up to him and hoping as always to learn some useful information which he could turn to his profit, he offered the accused man a drink from his flask. Blueskin accepted the drink and encouraged by Wild's apparent friendliness asked him to say a good word for him at his trial. Wild laughed in his face and said, "I can't do that. You're a dead man and will be tucked up very speedily."

Blueskin, enraged by his casual heartlessness, flew at him and drawing a penknife from his pocket he cut the thief-taker's throat to the windpipe. Wild fell back gurgling blood from his mouth, but fortunately for him two surgeons who stood nearby immediately came to his assistance and stitched him up before it was too late. Blueskin, apologizing for not having more efficiently dispatched "the viper," blamed the bluntness of his knife and the thickness of Wild's plaited muslin stock. He said that "he should be hang'd with Pleasure if Wilde did but die before him [and] that he was fully determin'd to murder him; and that his Intention was to have cut off his Head, and thrown it into the Sessions House Yard amongst the rabble and curs'd with many bloody oaths both his Hand and the Knife for not doing it effectually."

Wild survived, but Blueskin's attack was a warning which he would have done well not to disregard. In his limitless ambition and boundless confidence he was overreaching himself. He selected his victims without regard to their capacities for revenge or their popularity.

In tracking down Jack Sheppard he was pitting himself against the most popular criminal of his time and the consequences for him were disastrous. He caught Jack and brought him to trial, but within a few months he was brought to trial himself and convicted on evidence no more satisfactory than that upon which he had secured the conviction of Sheppard. No one who might have helped him came forward to do so. The judge who presided at his trial was Sir William Thompson, a corrupt lawyer and politician who hated Wild and who had helped to draft the law which had made it a capital offence to receive stolen goods and not prosecute the felon who stole them. It was for a minor breach of this law that Wild was sentenced to death, and the several witnesses who stood ready to charge him with more serious crimes, including murder, were consequently not required.

At two o'clock in the morning before his execution Wild took a dose of laudanum, but succeeded only in making himself delirious. He was, however, scarcely conscious of what was happening to him when he was bundled into the cart later on that morning. And he was lucky that it was so, for it was, apparently, "not easy to express with what roughness he was treated by the mob, not only as he went to the tree, but even when he was at it; instead of those signs of pity they generally show when common criminals are going to execution, they reviled and cursed him, and pelted him with stones and dirt continually."

CHAPTER EIGHT

NEWGATE

—

THE execution of Wild took place in the late spring of 1725, but when Mr. Kneebone called on the famous thief-taker in the summer of the year before, he was still at the height of his power. It took him less than forty-eight hours to catch Jack Sheppard and bring him to justice.

Since the burglary at Mr. Kneebone's house Jack, with his friend Blueskin Blake, had taken to the road.

He seems, in spite of his posthumous reputation, to have had little success as a highwayman and remained one only for a few days. On 19th July he and Blueskin stopped a carriage on the Hampstead road, but the sole occupant was a lady's maid from whom they were able to take no more than half a crown. The following evening they robbed Mr. Pargiter, a drunken grocer, as he staggered out of the Half Way House in Hampstead Village, but they were unlucky as the fellow had spent most of his weekly earnings in the inn and only had six shillings on him.* The next day they were scarcely more fortunate when they got away with twenty-two shillings from a stage coach. Before they could enjoy the profits of this minor triumph Edgworth Bess was arrested in a brandy shop near Temple Bar.

Wild had concentrated on finding her, believing that as soon as he did so he could make her tell him where her lover was hiding. Frightened by his threats of violence and the terrifying way he stared unfeelingly into her eyes, Bess told her tormentor that Jack was staying at the brandy shop kept by Blueskin's mother in Rosemary Lane. A few hours later Quilt Arnold, Wild's lieutenant, surprised Jack in his room. Jack fired at Arnold, but his pistol flashed in the pan and Arnold was able to take him and march him off to a magistrate who consigned him to Clerkenwell.

*On July 25th two brothers Benjamin and Francis Brightwell, "Grenadiers in the 2nd Company of Footguards," were charged with this crime on the evidence of the drunken Mr. Pargiter and were committed to Newgate. On hearing of their imprisonment Jack confessed to Mr. Wagstaff that he and Blueskin were responsible for the robbery. On August 13th the two "Centinels in the Guards" were acquitted, but soon afterwards one of them so shamed by the charge "broke his heart" and having contracted gaol fever "dy'd at his lodgings in the country." According to one of his officers, quoted by *The Daily Journal*, he was a remarkable man. "He was always reputed a Person of remarkable Sobriety, Justness, and Probity; . . . he was a Person extraordinarily well accomplish'd with Latin and Greek Literature and good skill in Roman Antiquities. . . . There was not such a Grenadier in the Universe, he carrying a large share of exquisite Learning under his Grenadier's Cap."

The next morning he was taken before Justice Black-erby and committed to Newgate.

Newgate was the largest and best known of the London prisons. It was also the oldest. There had been a prison on the site since the twelfth century and probably even earlier. In 1422 a licence was granted to the executors of Richard Whittington "to re-edify the gaol of Newgate." But by the end of the sixteenth century it was once more in ruins and had to be "new fronted and new faced." Soon after the restoration was completed, however, it was completely gutted in the Great Fire and had once again to be rebuilt.

The new prison finished in 1672 was designed "with great magnificence." The front of the archway facing Snow Hill bore "four emblematical figures viz. Liberty, Peace, Security and Plenty" and beneath them a statue of Dick Whittington and his cat to commemorate the interest which the celebrated Lord Mayor had taken in the jail. On the east front of the building were stone statues of Justice, Fortitude, and Plenty. The appearance was certainly grandiose and impressive, but "the sumptuous-ness of the outside but aggravated the misery of the wretches within," who lived behind those handsome decorated walls in conditions of ghastly squalor.

The stench inside was so appalling that even those who had becomed hardened to noxious smells by a lifetime spent in London could not enter certain parts of the prison without feeling sick. The suffocating and putrid fumes filled the atmosphere like a thick stagnant fog and during the epidemics of jail fever, a virulent form of typhoid, they bore the germ of the revolting disease into every cell of the prison. The foul and constant smell polluted what little food and water the prisoners could get hold of and impregnated their clothes and clung to their hair. It was everywhere and it was inescapable, revolting their nostrils and clogging their lungs, pervading their whole existence.

On entering the repulsive saturated atmosphere of Newgate or any other jail, the prisoner was immediately set upon by his fellow prisoners for what they called "garnish" or "chummage." This entailed emptying the pockets for the benefit of the other inmates of the ward into which the prisoner was put and of standing drinks all round. For drink was sold openly in prisons at the prison taproom or at a bar in the cellar. Those who could afford it deadened their senses by gin and lived out their sentences in a state of drunken stupor. The prison officials encouraged this excessive drinking and derived enormous profits from the sale of spirits, which was but one of their recognized perquisites. In the seventeenth century Sir Francis Mitchell, a Middlesex magistrate, had received a salary of £40 a year from the Keeper of Newgate "on condition of sending all his prisoners there" so that the profits on the sale of liquor might be increased. But Newgate in the eighteenth century was so crowded anyway that there was no longer any necessity for bribing magistrates to send in customers.

As prisoners came regularly in so the profits of the Keeper and his officials and turnkeys grew larger and larger. Apart from their profits on gin there was the profit on candles, which were necessary in the whole of the dark rambling prison even in daytime, and the profit on food and water. There were also the numerous authorized and unauthorized fees and fines which they were at liberty to impose upon their helpless charges.

The first fee which a prisoner might be expected to pay was for "easement of irons." The more a prisoner was willing to pay for this easement the less irksome his fetters would be. It had, therefore, become customary to weigh down a rich-looking new-comer with every conceivable handcuff, fetter, chain, and iron until he or some visitor paid the turnkey his fee for removing them. Having paid to be relieved of his irons the prisoner soon learned that his expenses did not stop there. Every day of his life in the jail he would be called upon to press a coin into the filthy palm of a turnkey for one reason or another. He would have to pay for the privilege of approaching the doubtful comforts of the sea-coal fire if there was one, for eating bread which was not stale, for drinking water which was not brackish, for having a blanket to keep himself warm, or for the privilege of not being whipped or tortured, whether he had done anything wrong or not.

His ability to pay would also govern the adequacy of his accommodation.

If he could pay well he might be allowed to sleep in the better part of the prison known as the Castle, where there was at least some light and air and where the beds were separated from each other by partitions. Living here, of course, was expensive and only the richest prisoners could afford it. The accommodation in the Castle and around the press yard, another more salubrious part of the jail, was well patronized during the time of the Jacobite risings, when Newgate was full of rich and noble prisoners. It was estimated that during three or four months in 1716 William Pitt, the Keeper of Newgate, cleared some £3,000 or £4,000 from his Jacobite prisoners "besides valuable presents given in private." Mr. Pitt had good reason to believe that by paying a thousand pounds for the Keepership he had got a bargain.

Even the less pleasant parts of the prison had their price and the cheapest bed in the whole place cost two shillings a week. The whole establishment was, in fact, run as an infinitely disgusting and corrupt lodging house.

The building was divided up into sections for the different classes of prisoners, the Master Debtors' side, the Common Debtors' side, the Master Felons' side, and so on; but the privileged prisoners, male and female, in each section, seem to have been at liberty to wander freely wherever they wished and their treatment, whichever ward they were in, depended not upon their status or crime but upon their pocket.

Money was all that mattered, the only answer to cruelty and injustice, the only criterion by which a prisoner was judged. Without money a prisoner was lost. A prison was not only, as Fielding observed, a "prototype of hell" but "one of the dearest places" on earth.

As soon as his poverty was proved by his failure to pay "garnish" a prisoner was stripped in a riotous manner and thrown into the degradation of a common ward, such as the Stone Hold at Newgate, which, according to a convict who had been there in 1724, was "a terrible stinking dark and dismal place situate underground into which no daylight can come. It was paved with stone; the prisoners had no beds and lay on the pavement whereby they endured great misery and hardship." They "suffer themselves to live far worse than swine and to speak the truth the Augean stable would bear no comparison to it for they are almost poisoned by their own filth, and their conversation is nothing but one continued course of swearing cursing and debauchery."

Lunatics stumbled about in the loathsome straw; rats and mice, almost tame, burrowed in the dirt and excrement; babies were born in dark corners and left there to die; men and women died of hunger and disease uncared for and unwanted; young girls gave their bodies up to anyone who could recompense them with a few scraps of

stale food; condemned women did the same for nothing
hoping to become pregnant and thus escape the gallows.*
Day after day the pattern of existence remained unchanged;
night was scarcely distinguishable from day; in winter
the prisoners shivered with cold; in summer they were
stifled with the heat; in all seasons they were hungry and
they died.

For most prisoners Newgate was a sort of transit
camp between the courthouse and the gallows or the
transportation ship, but for a few it was a home. Major
Bernardi, for instance, who died in Newgate in 1736 at
the age of eighty-two had been awaiting trial in the
prison for more than forty years. Other convicts sentenced
to terms of short imprisonment, unable to pay their way
out of the place when their terms expired, were known
to have remained there until they died.

The timeless monotony and squalor gave way on
occasions to scenes of grotesque horror such as the one
described by a prisoner in Newgate during the reign of
Charles II. "There lay," this prisoner observed, "in . . . a
closet near the room where we were lodged the quartered

*The women or wenches that are condemn'd to death, never fail to
plead they are with child (if they are old enough) in order to stop
execution until they are delivered. Upon this they are order'd to be
visited by Matrons; if the Matrons do not find them Quick, they are
sure to swing next Execution Day; but very often they declare that they
are with Child, and often too the poor Criminals are so indeed; for tho'
they came never so good Virgins into the Prison, they are a set of Wags
there that take Care of these matters.—*Travels Over England*, Misson
(1698), translated from the French (1719).

bodies of those men who had been executed some days before for a real or pretended plot; and the reason why their quarters lay there so long, was the relatives were all that while petitioning to have leave to bury them; which, at length, with much ado was obtained for the quarters, but not for the heads, which were ordered to be set up in some part of the City. I saw the heads when they were brought up to be boiled; the hangman fetched them in a dirty dust bucket. . .and setting them down among the felons, he and they made sport with them. They took them by the hair, flouting, jeering, and laughing at them; and then giving them some ill names boxed them in the ears and cheeks. Which done the hangman put them into his kettle, and parboiled them with Bay-salt and Cummin-seed. . .and this to keep off the fowls from seizing on them."

The degrading effects which such scenes and such company had upon a new prisoner are not difficult to imagine. Particularly as the only means by which he he could earn enough money to pay his way out of the prison if he arrived there penniless were by doing debasing jobs for other prisoners or by actively engaging in one or other of the profitable vices or crimes which were carried on so diligently in the unlit corners of the jail.

For the jail was a hive of criminal activity. Robberies were planned there, visitors from the underworld at large moved in and out, coins were brought in for clipping and blocks of metal for coining. The forger worked uninterrupted and the pickpockets practised their craft and gave lessons to others. Prostitutes male and female taught children the secrets of their trade and how to steal a watch or a wallet in the moment of climax.

Other prisons in London were no better than Newgate and some were a good deal worse.

The debtors in Newgate received, or were at least intended to receive, each day "one coarse household wheaten loaf" and were "also given a certain quantity of beef every week, in proportion to the number of debtors." But in other prisons the only allowance was stale "bread boiled in mere water" and in at least one jail there was no food allowance at all and water could be obtained only on payment. The prisoner lived solely on charity and "in the place of durance," a cellar six inches deep in water and with an open sewer running through it, fought "with the rats" for food thrown to them through the door. A Parliamentary Committee in 1729 reported that three hundred persons died in the Marshalsea prison in less than three months of a previous year and in 1729 in the same prison more than three hundred and fifty debtors were found dying of starvation.

The worst of these appalling prisons were privately owned and were hired out as businesses to keepers who made as much as they could out of them. The Duke of Portland owned a prison which he hired out at eighteen guineas a year to a man whose treatment of the prisoners was notorious. In the Bishop of Ely's prison the inmates, including women, were "chained down upon their backs upon a floor." In another jail the Debtor's Ward was called "The Shew" because the convicts begged for food by letting down their shoes on ropes from the windows. In Bridewell the President of the Court of Governors sat at a table presiding over the whipping of naked male and female prisoners. So long as he held the hammer in the air the flogging continued and only when he let it drop could the man on duty at the whipping post take a rest from his tiring labours. Once an officer confined in Knaresborough jail "took with him a dog to defend him from vermin, but the dog was soon destroyed and the prisoner's face much disfigured by them."

It was not until 1729 that the first efforts were made to alleviate the lot of the prison convict by the appointment of the Parliamentary Committee to "inquire into the State of the jails of the Kingdom, and report the same with their opinion thereupon to the House."

Hogarth's painting of a meeting of the Committee shows the instruments of torture which were part of the equipment of the officials of the Fleet prison. On the table in front of the members of the Committee are the tongs and fetters and spiked collars which were used indiscriminately not only on refractory prisoners but also upon those who would not or could not pay to have them removed. Standing at the head of the table and on the left of the picture are the infamous Bambridge, "the inhuman jailer" of the Fleet prison, and John Huggins, a previous Warden who had purchased his wardenship from the Earl of Clarendon, the owner of the prison, for five thousand pounds.

Although in the picture "villainy, fear and conscience are mixed in yellow and livid" on the countenance of Bambridge, in fact both he and Huggins appeared to have treated the members of the Committee with scant respect and to have considered their questions and the whole inquiry an unwarranted infringement of their right to run their business in their own way.

Bambridge, the Committee reported, "hath been guilty of the most notorious breaches of his trust, great extortions, and the highest crimes and misdemeanours in the execution of his . . . office; and hath arbitrarily and unlawfully loaded with irons, put into dungeons and destroyed prisoners for debt under his charge, treating them in the most barbarous and cruel manner, in high violation and contempt of the laws of this kingdom." A similar report was published on Huggins, whose inhuman treatment of a prisoner named Arne was cited as an example of the barbarous manner in which he too treated his victims.

Arne's clothes were stripped off him on his arrival in the Fleet as a punishment for being unable to pay garnish and he was thrown naked into a foul-smelling dungeon above the prison sewer. This dungeon, unlighted and unventilated, was his home for some days. Food was occasionally thrown down to him, and a fellow prisoner, pitying his poor shivering body, somehow managed to get him a mattress.

Arne endeavouring to escape the cold and stench in his cell climbed inside the mattress where the feathers stuck to his skin. One day, noticing the door of the dungeon open, he clambered out of his mattress and ran round the prison half crazy with fear and discomfort and hunger and looking, with his body covered with little white feathers like a repellent half-plucked bird. A turnkey caught him as he ran down a corridor and dragging him back to his dungeon threw him once more inside.

Shocked as the Committee members were by this and other stories and strongly worded as their reports were, it was not easy to arouse public opinion against the appalling conditions of prison life. Bambridge, although brought to trial, was twice acquitted by sympathetic juries and Huggins "afterwards lived in comfort to the age of ninety."

Few people yet thought of convicts as persons worthy of consideration, let alone of humane treatment. Prison reform was still a long way off and men like John Howard and Silas Told who agitated for it were considered cranks by their contemporaries.

The Newgate which Jack Sheppard entered in that July of 1724 was, and remained for more than a hundred years, "one of the foulest places in the world."

CHAPTER NINE

THE TRIAL

—

O N THE morning of 13th August after more than a fortnight spent in Newgate Jack was un-chained, his fetters were knocked off, and he was taken to the courthouse in Old Bailey to be tried for his life. The courthouse was a stark forbidding building on the south side of the prison and Jack admitted later that his heart fell as he was led into its grey interior, where the sounds of footsteps and voices echoed down the lofty corridors and where even the sunlight seemed cold and melancholy.

In the vast Justice Hall the tall chair of the Court President dominated the silent and depressing scene. Above the chair the statue of a stern relentless Justice looked towards the middle of the stone floor, where lonely and comfortless stood the prisoner's box.

Jack was already in the box when the officers of the court came into the Justice Hall. Sir Peter Delme, the

Lord Mayor, was followed by Sir William Thompson, the Recorder, and Serjeant Raby, the Recorder's deputy.

There were three indictments to consider. Jack was first accused of breaking into the house of William Phillips on 14th February and stealing "divers goods" in the night, but for lack of evidence he was soon acquitted. He was secondly indicted for breaking into the shop of Mary Cook on 5th February but of this charge also he was acquitted.

The third indictment concerned the Kneebone robbery and it was upon this charge that Jonathan Wild had concentrated his attention and upon which he hoped to secure a conviction.

The Clerk of Arraigns read the indictment to the court and then the Old Bailey attorney arose to face the Recorder.

"May it please your Lordship," he announced, "and you gentlemen of the jury, I am Counsel for the King against the prisoner at the bar."

No attorney rose to introduce himself as counsel for the defence, for it was considered in criminal trials of this kind the judge's duty to protect the prisoner.

Not for more than a hundred years was a prisoner charged with felony allowed to have counsel to cross-examine witnesses or to address the jury. Nor was he permitted to go into the witness box to give evidence on his own behalf, nor yet to see a copy of the evidence taken down in writing in the court where he had been committed for trial. The only hope for the prisoner was in what Lord Justice Mackinnon was later to call the "general conspiracy of benevolence on the part of judges, juries and counsel to mitigate the effects of the system by excessive technicalities of procedure."

It was not unknown, for instance, for a prisoner to be acquitted by a sympathetic court because of some trifing inaccuracy in the indictment, such as the misspelling of his name. Nor was it unknown for a capital charge to be quashed by reason of the prosecutor or jury committing what Blackstone termed "pious perjury" and undervaluing the articles stolen so that the crime was no longer a capital one. A pleasant story is told of a prosecutor who, angered by his stolen watch being valued at a fraction of its cost, exclaimed that "the fashion alone cost me more than that." "Come, sir," replied the judge, "we cannot hang a man for fashion's sake."

This "conspiracy of benevolence" did not, of course, always operate and Jack Sheppard, as he faced his accusers and the three principal witnesses who had been prepared by the prosecution, was virtually defenceless.

The first witness called by the Counsel for the King was the prosecutor himself.

"The prisoner," Mr. Kneebone deposed, "had sometime been my servant. On the morning of 13th June, all having been fast the previous night, I found the bar of my Cellar Window was cut, the Bolts of my Cellar-Door were drawn, and the padlock wrenched off; the shutter in my shop was broke, and 108 yards of Woolen Cloth (etc.)...were taken away. I presently suspected the Prisoner, because he had lately committed some ill Actions in the Neighbourhood; and acquainting Jonathan Wild with it, by his means the Prisoner was apprehended, and committed to Prison. I went to see him there, and asked him how he could be so ungrateful as to rob me, after I had shewn him so much kindness? He confest he had been very ungrateful in doing so, but said he had been drawn into it by ill Company."

The second witness was Jonathan Wild. He corroborated Mr. Kneebone's having asked him for help and said,"I promised to do him all the service I could, and accordingly, understanding that the Prisoner was acquainted with Joseph Black, alias Blueskin, and William Field, I sent for Field, who coming to me, I told him if he would make an ingenious Confession I believed I could prevail with the Court to admit him as an evidence." Field then, according to Wild, did make such a confession and told him where the cloth was hidden.

It was now left for the Old Bailey attorney to call William Field. If Field repeated his confession convincingly in open court the case would be complete.

The witness stood up and began his evidence fluently and confidently.

"The Prisoner told me and Blueskin that he knew of a *Ken* worth *Milling*—that is a *House* worth *Breaking*—for he said there was something good to be got in it.... Blueskin and I disapproved of the Design, because we did not think it could easily be done; but the Prisoner told us it might be done with all the Pleasure in Life, for he had lived there with the Prosecutor, and was acquainted with every part of the House, and he would undertake it himself, if we would but stand where we were, and give a good Look out. We agreeing to this, he cut the bar of the Cellar and Window, and so got into the Shop, and brought out three Parcels of Cloth which we carried away."*

Wild's witness had done his work well. There could be no doubt now of the outcome of the trial. The members of the Jury retired for a few moments only.

---

*It is interesting and revealing to compare Field's evidence on this occasion with his evidence at Blueskin's trial in the following October. On one of these occasions he was lying and probably on both. At Blueskin's trial he was as anxious to make it appear that Blueskin was the instigator of the crime as he was at Sheppard's to give the impression that the burglary was Sheppard's idea. His evidence when he was helping Wild to obtain the conviction of Blueskin was that he was "not much acquainted" with Sheppard. "I had," he went on to say, "seen him but two or three Times, by Means of his coming to my House in the Mint. The Prisoner asked me to go out with him and Sheppard to rob Mr. Kneebone. I was unwilling to expose myself to any Danger, and told him that I did not know the House. 'Blood!' says he. 'Nor I neither; but Jack Sheppard does, for he has lived there, and he'll undertake it, and we shall have nothing to do but to help to carry off the Goods, or else I should be as unwilling to venture as you.'"

"Do you find the prisoner guilty or not guilty?" the Recorder asked them when they returned.

It was a formal question asked without apparent interest, with little doubt as to its answer.

"Guilty," the foreman of the jury immediately replied.

Jack was marched back to the prison between two turnkeys and was chained down once more to the stone floor of his cell.

The following morning he and fifty-five other prisoners were taken back again to the Justice Hall to hear the Recorder announce their sentences. Nine prisoners, who were guilty of comparatively minor offences, were sentenced to be burned in the hand; thirty-one were ordered for transportation; six were condemned to death. Two of those condemned to death were paltry highwaymen, one was a burglar, another was a shoplifter, a fifth was a woman who had taken some money out of a club box. The last was Jack Sheppard.

The six capital prisoners were told to hold out their hands to the hangman whose savage and traditional duty it was to tie their thumbs together with whipcord.

With the whipcord tied agonisingly round his thumbs and cutting the flesh to the bone Jack was led back once more to his prison cell.

CHAPTER TEN

THE CONDEMNED HOLD*

JACK, on his return to Newgate, was put into the Condemned Hold, a dismal cell adjoining the Lodge and close to the prison gate. The floor was of stone and a wide wooden shelf with a row of ring bolts above it served as a communal bed for the condemned prisoners. The small and narrow windows faced on to the lane beneath the arch and let into the cold forbidding cell as little air as light.

On the orders of Bodenham Rouse, the Deputy Keeper, Jack was heavily chained and fettered, but was allowed the customary privilege enjoyed by the other capital prisoners of going up to the thick wooden partition to talk to their visitors in the Lodge.

*During some of the events recorded in this and subsequent chapters Sheppard is on occasions on his own and there is no corroborative evidence for the details which I have given. I have taken it that these details, which Sheppard himself subsequently gave to Defoe and Wagstaff, are correct. There is no reason to suppose that they are not.

The Lodge, which was a sort of reception room for the prison, was also used by the turnkeys as a meeting-place and bar. Mrs. Spurling, the widow of a turnkey, former head of the prison, was in charge of the bar and spent most of her time in the Lodge, drinking with her late husband's colleagues. Mr. Spurling had been calmly and deliberately shot by a butcher turned highwayman in the courtyard of the Old Bailey Session House when he refused to allow the highwayman permission to talk to a woman accused of coining. The woman clapped her hands as she watched the turnkey die and congratulated his murderer on his good shot. But that was some twelve years previously and Mr. Spurling's widow, a fat and jovial woman, had had plenty of time to regain her former cheerful conviviality. She and her companions usually sat at a table at the far end of the Lodge facing the gate, where they could keep an eye upon those who came in and went out and upon the stout partition, topped by its menacing *chevaux de frise*, behind which the prisoners in the Condemned Hold waited for the day of execution.

During the last week in August Jack's "dead warrant" was sent to the prison. September 4th was the day appointed in the warrant for his hanging and this gave him less than a week to make his escape. He had already discussed with his three companions in the Hold a plan of escape which seemed feasible, but preparations for putting this plan into execution had been abandoned when his confederates received news from friends of a possible reprieve and when Jack fell ill of a fever. It was not until the evening before the day appointed for their execution that the three men learned that their hopes of escaping the gallows were unjustified. The efforts to obtain a reprieve had failed.

Davis, one of the three condemned men, realizing that it was now too late to make his escape, gave Jack the tools which his friends had smuggled in to him. Jack had fully recovered from his illness and as soon as he had said good-bye to Davis and wished him a quick and painless death, he set to work with his file on one of the spikes which were ranged along the top of the partition separating the Condemned Hold from the Lodge. He worked all day at his filing, stopping only when a visitor or a turnkey passed through the Lodge or entered the Hold. By the evening of the following day he had got more than half-way through the spike and he believed that another day's work would so weaken it that he would be able, at any time he wanted to, to break it off with his hand.

The next day, unfortunately, was Sunday and the crowds of visitors passing in and out of the Lodge all day made it impossible for him to complete his task, and he dared not do so during the relative quiet of the night for fear of being heard by the turnkey who stayed on duty at the desk on the far side of the partition. On the Monday morning, however, when the noisy life of the prison began again he went back to the spike and started filing once more.

At midday Edgworth Bess and her friend Poll Maggot came to visit him and all afternoon as they talked and laughed with him he tirelessly continued with his work. By six o'clock he had snapped the spike off and had thereby made a gap in the *chevaux de frise*, only about nine inches square, but just large enough, he thought, for his extraordinarily supple body to squeeze through.

Taking a quick glance at the turnkeys chatting and drinking as they sat around the table to her right, Bess pushed a nightgown and a bonnet through the gap at the top of the partition. Jack quickly put them on and, catching hold of the two spikes on either side of the gap he had made, he pulled himself up on to the top of the partition, and, helped by the two girls, he wriggled through and lowered himself down into the Lodge.

In full view of the turnkeys, while Poll hid herself as best she could in an angle which the partition made with the wall of the Lodge, Jack and Bess walked slowly across to the prison gate. The turnkeys "engag'd in a deep Discourse concerning his Dexterity in his formerly escaping from New-Prison" and the methods they themselves would have used to prevent it, noticed nothing amiss. Two girls had come in to visit Sheppard and now apparently two girls were going out, chattering and laughing as before.

Immediately they had reached the street without being questioned, Jack and Bess ran to a coach which was waiting for them at the top of Old Bailey. This coach, hired by William Page, a butcher's young son and a friend and passionate admirer of Jack, had been waiting there all afternoon. Jack, greeted excitedly by the devoted Page, leapt into the coach with Bess and was driven off quickly to Blackfriars Stairs, where Poll, who had walked unnoticed out of the prison when she was sure that the other two had got safely away, arrived a few minutes later to meet them.

The four excited fugitives took a boat to Westminster Horse Ferry. The waterman later confessed that he saw Jack's "Irons under his Night-Gown and was much terrified thereat." So terrified in fact that he accepted the sevenpence Jack offered him without daring to question him or to attempt to prevent his escape. His passengers stepped out onto the other bank of the river and made their way to the White Hart alehouse, where they all celebrated with a bottle of brandy.

Jack and Bess then moved on to another inn at Holborn and there in a back room Jack sawed off his chains and, free once more, cheerful and slightly drunk, he took his mistress off to sleep with her in a room in Spitalfields.

Meanwhile the jailers, harassed by the Sheriff for what *The Daily Journal* was later to call "the most surprising Accident at Newgate," and insulted by the balladmongers, enlisted the help of Jonathan Wild, promising him a good reward and a percentage of their future profits if he succeeded in recapturing him. Wild accepted the commission and on the afternoon of the following day he

secured the arrest of Edgworth Bess and had her committed to the Poultry Compter, where he and his
colleagues "terrified and purged her as much as was
possible," in order to force her to divulge Jack's where-
abouts. But she in spite of this treatment insisted, either
heroically or in real ignorance, that she had no idea where
he was and her torturers, realizing that they might be
wasting their time, left her in prison in case she should
change her mind, and set off to follow other scents which
they hoped might lead them to their quarry.

On 4th September, the day appointed for Jack's
execution, they arranged for an advertisement to appear
in the Press."Whereas," the advertisement ran,"John
Shepheard broke out of the Condemn'd Hold of Newgate
(with his Irons on) by cutting off one of the large Iron
Spikes over the Main Door on Monday the 31st of
August last, about six a clock in the Evening, he is about
23 years of Age and about five Foot four Inches high, very
slender, and of a pale Complection, has lately been very
sick, did wear a light Bob Wig, a light colour'd Cloth
Coat, and white Waistcoat, has an impediment in his
speech and is a Carpenter by Trade. Whoever will discover or apprehend him so that he be brought to Justice
shall receive 20 guineas Reward to be paid by the
Keeper of Newgate."

Jack had, however, by this time got well away.
Provided by Page with a butcher's blue smock and
woollen apron and some money taken from old Mr.Page's

till, he and his young friend had got out of London on the road to Oxford looking like two innocent butcher's apprentices on a walk in the country.

They were making for the village of Chipping Warden in Northamptonshire, where Page had an old aunt and uncle who kept a small holding and where he thought Jack would be safe for a few days until the excitement died down and the heat of the chase cooled off.

On their safe arrival in Chipping Warden they were welcomed by the kindly old couple, who seemed delighted to see their nephew again and gave him and his friend a good meal and a comfortable bed. But Jack and Page soon grew tired of country life and after three or four days, feeling they could not in any case impose any longer upon the hospitality of their generous but impoverished host, they decided to make their way back to London.

They arrived in London again with only a shilling left between them on the afternoon of 8th September, but the hopes they had of their return being unnoticed were disappointed when on passing through Drury Lane on their way to Bishopsgate, Jack was recognized by a milkman who came up to talk to him. Jack, unable to avoid the meeting, made the milkman promise that he would keep to himself Jack's "incognito return to the Metropolis."

As soon as Jack was out of sight, however, the milkman lost no time in telling everyone he knew that Jack Sheppard was back in London and "the news like infection soon spread over the Hundreds of Drury." An hour or so after his unfortunate meeting with the milkman Jack was recognized again as he sat drinking with Page in Cooley's brandy shop in Bishopsgate Street. A cobbler, who rented a stable in the yard of the brandy shop, came into the bar for a drink, but stopped short on seeing Jack and stood hesitantly in the doorway apparently considering what his chances would be of getting hold of a constable and claiming the reward offered on the felon's conviction. A sympathetic customer in the bar guessing what the cobbler had in mind went over to Jack and whispered a warning in his ear. Jack left immediately and moved on to the Cock and Pye alehouse where he and Page spent their few remaining pennies on a dishful of oysters and a quartern of brandy. While eating the oysters, a barber who knew Jack slightly came up to him and told him that the milkman he had met earlier on that evening in Drury Lane had passed round the news of his return so industriously that there could be few people in the district who did not by now know of it, and fewer still who had not been made familiar with Jack's appearance by the leaflets giving his description which had been distributed in hundreds all over London.

Jack, enraged by the milkman's treacherous stupidity, straight away left for the cellar where he lived and finding the door locked he tore it off its hinges. Then lifting it up above his head he hurled it down the cellar steps into the darkness below "causing a deluge of cream and milk all over the cellar." The milkman crouching on his bed in a corner was, he afterwards confessed, so terrified by the sudden appalling din of the crash of the pails and upset churns that, feeling all the milk splashing around him, he thought for a moment that a murdered body had been thrown down at his feet and he mistook the milk for blood.

Jack, feeling calmer after this violent outburst, now devoted his attention to the problem of getting hold of some money. Previously that evening he and Page had passed by the window of Mr. Martin's the watchmaker's shop in Fleet Street opposite St. Bride's Church and had admired there the gold and silver watches on display. Now that it was getting late he went back to the Cock and Pye alehouse for Page and together they paid a further visit to the watchmaker.

When the street was quiet and the passers-by few and far between, Jack screwed a gimlet into the doorpost while Page kept a look-out up and down the street. As soon as he had screwed in the gimlet as far as it would go he tied a length of packthread to it and passed the other end of the thread through the door-knocker so that if the shopboy heard them smashing the window he would be unable to get out of the shop to give the alarm. That the shopboy was that night left in sole charge of his shop they had already discovered on their previous visit, when Page had been inside to ask if a Mr. Taylor was the owner of the premises and on being told he was not stayed for a few minutes' conversation.

Having made the door fast with the piece of thread

Jack hurled a stone through the glass and a few seconds
later, followed hot-foot by Page, he was racing down
Fleet Street with fifteen pounds' worth of watches in his
pockets. They got clear away, but later on that night
they were seen by Ireton, one of the under-turnkeys at
Newgate, strolling down Drury Lane. With a shout
Ireton chased after them, but in the darkness he mistook
Page for Jack and grabbed hold of the wrong body while
his intended quarry threw himself under a nearby coach.
Realizing his mistake Ireton let Page go, but the delay
had given Jack a chance to get away too and although his
pursuer called out every constable in the district he did
not catch another sight of him.

After this narrow escape Jack decided that he had
come back to London sooner than he should. The town
was still too hot for him. Joining up with Page again,
who seems to have found him more quickly than a parish-
ful of constables could, he moved out of the town to
Finchley Common and sheltered in an isolated and
deserted cottage where he stayed with Page the whole
day of 9th September.

The following day a posse of turnkeys, having received
information which led them to suspect that the two
fugitives were hiding on the Common, rode out to beat
it from end to end. They were determined to catch their
prey, not only for the sake of the reward which was
offered for his capture but also because they had been
accused of conniving at Sheppard's escape and accepting

large bribes from his friends to ensure his continued freedom. It was an accusation which they were anxious to
prove false. William Pitt, the Keeper of Newgate, although ill at this time, had recently been tried twice on
charges of accepting bribes from rich prisoners and
allowing them to escape. He had been acquitted, but his
assistants knew more than they had admitted at the trials
and were consequently very uneasy about what might
come out at a future inquiry and interfere with a useful
source of income.

Jack and Page hiding in their cottage saw the line of
turnkeys approaching from the south and slipped out of
the cottage by the back door. They crept along a hedge-
row, but as they did so they were spotted by Langley, one
of the turnkeys, who galloped towards them. Jack shouted
a warning to Page, who, being neither as nimble and wily
nor as experienced as Jack, was soon caught. Jack, however, dashed headlong into a copse and once more gave
his pursuers the slip. After lying low in the copse for a
few hours he made his way towards a group of farm
buildings near Brown's Hall, and tired and hungry he
crawled into a pile of straw in the stable and went to sleep.

Towards midday the turnkeys rode into the farmyard,
and, followed by a young dairymaid who was excited by
the commotion, they began to search the buildings. Two
of them went into the stable and seeing nothing to arouse
their suspicions they were on the point of going out again
when the dairymaid pointed excitedly to a pair of boots

sticking out of the stack of straw in the corner. The
turnkeys pounced on the boots and pulled Jack out by his
ankles.

Calling in their companions to see their captive, they
searched him diligently and took away from him two of
the stolen watches, which he was concealing under his
armpits, some money and a knife. And then, delighted at
their success, they bound Jack's wrists behind his back and
carried him off to a nearby inn to celebrate their capture.
As they entered the inn Jack noticed hanging above the
doorway the inn sign which bore the legend "I have
brought my hogs to a fair market," and comparing himself good-humouredly to a greedy hog, Jack asked for a
large measure of brandy which the turnkeys, amused by
his apparent unconcern and cheerful mood, willingly gave
him. Laughing and joking together they stayed drinking
in the inn for some time and "were all merry together."

On their return journey to London they hired a coach
on the outskirts of the town in which to convey the
prisoner back to Newgate. The coach arrived outside the
prison gate at about two o'clock and Jack, who had been
watching all the time for a chance to escape, jumped out
of the carriage as soon as the door was opened and darting
underneath it made a dash to escape on the far side. He was
soon caught, however, and led into Newgate, where he
was once more incarcerated in the Condemned Hold, but
this time he was chained to the floor and guarded so that
escape should be unthinkable. Young Page was locked

up in a different cell where he could be of no further assistance to his friend.*

It was a gala night in Newgate. Bumper after bumper was drunk to celebrate the recapture of the famous criminal. A sing-song began with the Te Deum and ended with ribald ballads. The first sightseers were admitted into the Hold to see the chained Sheppard at a cost of three and sixpence a head. At the height of the festivities when almost the entire staff of the prison and many of the prisoners were incapably drunk, news was delightedly received that the hated Jonathan Wild had followed a false scent as far as Stourbridge. At least one prisoner literally laughed himself sick.

Outside the prison that night and throughout the following week Sheppard was the chief topic of conversation, the main source of interest in the town. "His escape and his being so suddenly retaken made such a noise in the town that it was thought all the common people would have gone mad about him; there being not a porter to be had for love nor money, nor getting into an alehouse, for butchers, shoemakers and barbers all engaged in controversies and wagers about Sheppard." It was in fact, so

*Sheppard steadfastly refused to incriminate Page, "carefully guarded himself against uttering anything that might affect him," and took "great pains to excuse [him] of being in any way privy to his Crimes." On 4th December, however, Page was tried at the Old Bailey Sessions on charges of being Sheppard's accomplice in robbing Mr. Martin's shop and of "receiving, comforting and harbouring" Sheppard after his escape. He was found guilty on both indictments and sentenced to transportation.

the journalist claimed, "a week of the greatest noise and idleness among mechanics that has been known in London."

Newgate was "night and day surrounded with the curious and Tyburn road daily lined with women and children, and the gallows as carefully watched by night lest he should be hanged incog."

This nervous anxiety that Sheppard might be hanged secretly to avoid a riot was not calmed down until *The Daily Journal* published a notice to the effect that "John Sheppard, the notorious Malefactor, having escap'd from Justice after his conviction and Sentence, we are now assured, that it must be proved in a regular and judicial Way that he is the same person who was so convicted, and escaped, before a fresh order can be made for his Execution, and that this Matter will come before the Court at the Old-Bailey the next Sessions." And so the excitement for the moment abated and the people waited impatiently for the next appearance of the "notorious Malefactor" before his judges.

CHAPTER ELEVEN

THE GREAT ESCAPE
FROM NEWGATE

═══

WHEN the information that a new trial would be necessary reached Newgate, Jack was taken from the Condemned Hold to the Castle, a cell high up on the third floor above the prison gate and believed to be the strongest and most impregnable part of the whole prison.

Here Jack was, as before in the Hold, chained down to the floor, and fettered. He offered the usual fee for easement of irons, but his jailers had orders to refuse the fee and in no circumstances to allow him to be released from his chains for any reason at all.

As money was of no use to him he asked his visitors and friends to bring him tools so that, as he could not buy his way out of his irons, he might force his way out of them. Within a few days he was brought a small watchmaker's file which he was able to conceal in a Bible which the prison chaplain had given him and which was the only thing he was allowed to have near him when he was alone. He made some headway with the padlocks by means of this file, but just as he was beginning to get the hang of them, his file was discovered by the chaplain who, taking the Bible from him one day, found it concealed between the pages and handed it over to a turnkey.

Some time after this Jack was supplied with several stronger and more useful tools including some nails, a hammer, two files, and a chisel which he managed to hide between the rushes of the seat of a chair which was provided in the cell for the use of visitors and jailers. With the help of these tools Jack was able to escape completely from his irons and made a practice to walk about his cell of an evening "for the ease of his legs."

One evening as he strolled about his cell taking his customary exercise, he was surprised by a turnkey who came in unexpectedly with a meal for him at an irregular time.

The turnkey looked in amazement at Jack, who greeted him as if his wandering about the cell was the most natural thing in the world." 'Twas troublesome," the prisoner complained with a disarming lack of emphasis, "to be always in one posture."

After Jack had been secured once more the turnkey sent for Mr. Pitt, the Keeper, now recovered from his illness, and his deputies so that it could be decided how the tiresome fellow could be more effectively confined.

While the officials were discussing their problem Jack asked them if they would like a demonstration of how he had managed to release himself from his irons. They watched in amazement as the extraordinary youth used his tools with such remarkable strength and skill, amounting to a "Magick Art," that he was free again within a few minutes.

Pitt immediately gave orders for the felon to be loaded with even heavier irons and a larger and unbreakable padlock, and for his movements to be further restricted by encircling his wrists in an enormous pair of handcuffs.

No prisoner, so far as one of the chaplains could recall, had ever been so heavily ironed before. William Kneebone, who had arrived on one of his regular visits to Jack as the handcuffs were being padlocked, interceded for his former shopboy with tears in his eyes. He was, in spite of the recent robbery, for which Jack appeared genuinely sorry, still very fond of the boy and felt a regretful responsibility for his present hopeless condition. His earnest pleadings and offered bribes did not, however, have any effect upon the jailers, who not only feared the consequences of another escape but who were anxious not to lose so profitable an exhibit.

And so for the next week Jack languished in acute discomfort in his cell, sometimes lifting himself up to sit in a chair, more often lying down on his back on the stone floor. The visitors who still flocked in scores to see him

noticed with pity the raw scars round his wrists where
the iron of the handcuffs had cut his skin and gave him
money for which he had no use and which he immediately
sent away to other prisoners who were able to buy themselves some degree of comfort with it.

Without an implement of any kind to pick the locks
which fastened the heavy chains around him he was unable
even to attempt an escape. Visitors were now carefully
watched by the turnkeys to see that they did not pass him
any tools which would, as he later said, have been "more
useful to him"at that time"than all the mines of Mexico."
And then one day during the second week of October a
friend was able without being seen to leave within Jack's
reach on the floor of the cell before he left it an old and
rusty but strong and useful nail. If the turnkey noticed the
nail, which is unlikely, he disregarded it and when Jack
was alone he was able to stretch out and pick it up and
hide it in his stocking.

On 14th October the Old Bailey Sessions began and
for the next few days Jack knew that the turnkeys would
be busier than ever with a full prison and with the addi-
tional duty of escorting prisoners backwards and forwards from the Sessions House. If he was to escape at all,
now was his chance.

At about two o'clock on 15th October Jack's dinner
was as usual brought to him by William Austin, one of
his jailers. Jack set to with a good appetite and Austin
sat down in the cell to talk to him while he was eating.

Before he had finished Captain Geary of New Prison and Mr. Gough of Westminster Gate-House, together with one or two other prison officials who were giving evidence at the Old Bailey Sessions, called in to see the famous thief. The prisoner and his visitors laughed and joked together until nearly three o'clock, when Austin stood up to take away Jack's empty plate and to make his usual careful examination of the handcuffs, fetters, and padlocks. Before leaving him Austin asked Jack to let him know now if there was anything he wanted because he would be too busy to come back again to see him until the following morning. Jack affected both annoyance and disappointment at this and begged Austin, if he really had no time to call in to see him again that evening, to be sure to come good and early in the morning because he was so lonely lying there by himself in the dark with nothing to occupy his mind.

Austin nodded and with a final glance at Jack's chains left the cell, locking and bolting the great door behind him. Jack listened for the rattle of the key in the lock and then set immediately to work.

There were, he guessed, no more than two hours of daylight left and he was determined to do as much as he could before it was dark. First of all he escaped from his handcuffs by means of the nail which he had kept concealed in his stocking. He clenched this nail firmly between his teeth and using it with practised dexterity he picked the lock. Then using the same nail he opened the immense horse padlock which secured the chain round his ankles to the staple in the floor. He was free now to hop about the cell, but there seemed at first sight no chance of breaking the chain which still linked his ankles together. On examining the chain, however, he found a link which appeared weaker than the rest and by twisting the chain backwards and forwards between his legs so that the weak link was further damaged by the strain which his frantic strength brought to bear on it, suddenly it broke and he was free. He was, of course, unable to squeeze his feet through the thick iron collars which encircled his ankles and to which the ends of the broken chain were still attached, so taking off his stockings he used them to bind up the links of the chain round his legs.

He had already decided that the only possible way of getting out of the prison was by climbing up the chimney into the room above and from there making his way onto the roof. The narrowness of the barred window ruled out any chance of escape by that means and although he could, he knew, break open the door of his cell, having done so he would still be on the same floor of the prison. Furthermore, opposite that door was the door leading to the quarters occupied by the Master Debtors, who would certainly hear him and might unintentionally betray him to the turnkeys.

Having already, during one of his nightly peregrinations the week before, poked his head up the chimney he knew that across the flue about six feet above the level of the floor was a thick square iron bar the ends of which were buried into the brickwork of the chimney on either side. This had obviously been built into the chimney to prevent prisoners escaping by squeezing up the flue as Jack intended to do. There was nothing to do then but to pull down the chimney brick by brick. So setting to work with the broken link he scratched away at the mortar joints until he had at last worked one brick loose. The job was not so difficult now and by means of his broken link and the horse padlock which he used as a sledge hammer he soon had a pile of bricks and mortar at his feet and the thick iron bar in his hands. Taking the bar with him he clambered up the chimney and using the end of it as a battering ram he smashed his way through into the room above.

This was a rectangular room measuring about twenty feet by ten feet, known as the Red Room, which had not been entered or used since 1716, when some rebels had been imprisoned there after the defeat of the Lancashire Jacobites at Preston. Dust lay thick on the floor, but Jack, who was by this time covered in brick and mortar dust himself, noticed nothing as he climbed through the hole that he had made, for it was by now pitch dark. From now on he was working in complete darkness. No light from the new moon came through the small prison windows and he had, of course, no means of making a light for himself. With his finger-tips on the walls he felt his way round the cell to the door and on the way his foot struck against a large nail which he picked up and put into the pocket of his apron, with his broken link and the other nail, in case he should later find a use for it. Soon he came to the door and with expert sensitive fingers he felt around its edges for the lock box. Using his three makeshift implements he had, within less than a quarter of an hour, bent aside the plate covering the lock box, picked the lock, and forced back the bolt. The door creaked open on its rusty hinges and Jack walked out into the passage.

He turned left past a staircase and came to another locked door, the door to the chapel. Turning aside for a moment from this door he felt his way around the passage in an attempt to find an easier way of getting up onto the next floor. But there was no other way out of the passage and he came back eventually to the chapel door. Once more he felt its surface and ran his finger-tips round its edges, but this door appeared to have no lock and it was bolted on the far side by a bolt which he could not budge. It seemed very quiet in this part of the prison and he decided to take the risk of battering a hole in the brick-work beside the door. He knocked and rammed the wall, making a frightening noise in the darkness, but no one heard him and soon he had made a hole large enough to get his arm through. Pushing his hand through this hole in the wall he felt for the bolt on the far side and pulled it back. He passed through into the chapel.

The chapel, which he knew only too well, was a

macabre and forbidding room divided by high partitions topped by iron spikes into separate pens for the different classes of prisoner. It was on the top floor of the prison and there was another door at its far side leading to the passage which gave access to the roof. To reach this door Jack smashed his way through into the pen reserved for prisoners condemned to death. He had been in this pen before and the curious distasteful smell of it, and of the whole chapel around it, was unpleasantly familiar to him. He was reminded of the horrifying sermons which the prison ordinary preached from his safe pulpit in a voice full of gloom and malice. He was determined to waste no time in the dreadful place. Although he could not see them he remembered the spikes that were ranged above him along the top of the partition and standing on top of a replica of a coffin, placed there to remind the convicts of their terrible fate, and grasping his iron bar firmly in both hands he hit furiously at one of the spikes until he had knocked it off. Then climbing up onto the top of the partition in the gap he had made in the row of spikes, he jumped down onto the far side. Putting the broken-off spike into his apron pocket with his other tools, he felt his way forward to the next door. When he had reached it it took him only a few seconds to discover that it was going to be the most difficult door of them all so far. He tried without success for more than half an hour to pick the lock, but his old rusty nails were neither thin nor pliable enough and the lock was a strong one. Eventually changing his tactics he was able with his bar and spike to lever the lock box far enough aside and to pick the lock from the inside. The door rattled on its hinges and pushing it open he hurried along the passage to the door at the far end.

When he touched this door his heart fell. The immense iron plated lock box was clamped to the door by iron hoops and beneath the lock box an enormous bolt was fastened into its socket by a hasp secured by a strong padlock. The door itself was strengthened by four vast metal fillets.

He had broken through four stout doors, and beyond this one was the roof. He was nearly free. But he was tired out and to break through this fifth door, heavier and better secured than any of the others, in complete darkness and without proper tools, seemed even to him impossible. For a moment he hesitated wondering what to do and then he heard the clock bells of St. Sepulchre's Church chiming the hour. He counted the chimes. Only eight o'clock. The thought that he had come so far in five hours and that he still had the whole night before him put new hope into him. He picked up his bar and with skill and determination attacked the door. Deciding that the lock could not be picked and the bolt could not be forced, he concentrated on the colossal metal fillet to which they were both attached. After long and anguished efforts he managed to force his bar into a position in which he could use it as a lever, and then applying to the end of his lever his frenzied and scarcely human strength he wrenched it from the door. The lock and the bolt were torn away with it.

He pulled the massive door open and walked along the corridor towards the roof. The door at the end of the corridor was bolted only on the inside, so having found the bolt he shot it back and came out gratefully onto the roof and into the fresh and sweet night air.

He was now on top of the gateway and many floors above the Lodge from which he had made his last escape. Surrounding him on every side were high walls shutting off his escape. Emptying his pockets he climbed up onto the top of the door which he had just opened and from there leapt to the top of the wall. He jumped down on the far side to the lead roof beneath, and crawling across the tiled roof of the Common Felons' ward, he came to the parapet wall of the gateway. Now for the first time he could see below him the houses and shops in Newgate Street. The shops were still open and the lights from the houses shone out into the street. The roofs of the houses were, he judged, about twenty-five feet below the place where he knelt and were too far away for him to jump down to them. Reluctantly he decided that he would have to go back for his blankets, so leaving the relative security of the roof he made his way back through the prison towards his cell. Feeling his way in the darkness he passed carefully but swiftly through the shattered door into the grotesque and silent chapel, along the stone corridors to

the Red Room where the disturbed dust had settled
mustily back onto the floor, and down the chimney into
his cell where the great pile of broken bricks lay heaped
in front of the fireplace, expecting all the time for a door
to open suddenly, for his escape to be noticed, his plan
to fail.

Quickly he picked up his blankets and clambering up
the chimney again he lost no time in getting back onto
the roof. No one saw him. He sat against the parapet
wall and tied his blankets together to make a rope. Then
having driven the spike from the chapel into the wall, he
tied the end of his blanket round it and climbed down
onto the roof below.

He crawled quietly across the slates until he came to
an attic window. There was no light inside and as he
pressed his hand against the unlocked window it gave
way and he climbed inside into the garret. He crept to
the door and waited there listening for a few moments and
then, hearing no sound, he opened it and went stealthily
down two flights of stairs onto the first floor landing. As
he moved to the head of the next flight of stairs the links
of one of the chains round his legs clanked. He stood
quite still where he was as he heard a woman's voice ask
in alarm: "Lord! what was that?" Still not moving he
heard the gruff less distinct voice of a man replying:
"Only a dog or a cat."

Thinking it was unsafe to go any farther until the
household had settled down for the night, he went back

The Castle

The Red Room

Door of the Red Room

Door going into the Chapel

*First Door between the Chapel
and the Leads*

*Second Door in the same
Passage*

Jack Sheppard escaping from Newgate

From illustrations based on contemporary prints by George
Cruikshank to *Jack Sheppard* by W. Harrison Ainsworth, 1839

Lower Leads

The Highest Leads and the Leads of the Turner's House

Jack Sheppard escaping from Newgate

From illustrations based on contemporary prints by George
Cruikshank to *Jack Sheppard* by W. Harrison Ainsworth, 1839

to the attic room which he had just left and locking the door behind him he threw himself on the bed in complete exhaustion and slept for two hours.

He was awakened by the sound of opening doors and voices on a lower floor and getting up again he crept once more downstairs. He heard the voices more clearly now saying good-bye to a guest in the hall and the front door opening and closing. He decided to make a run for it. Making sure his fetters were securely tied he rushed silently downstairs across the hall and through the front door into Newgate Street. He left the door wide open behind him and later on at midnight Mr. Bird and his family were knocked up by a watchman who found it open. Mr. Bird blamed the carelessness of a servant and went back unsuspectingly to bed.

Meanwhile Jack was walking unhurriedly across London. He had strolled past St. Sepulchre's watch-house and had wished the watchman good night. By way of Snow Hill and the Fleet Bridge he had made his way up Holborn Hill and was now heading for the open country beyond Gray's Inn Lane. By two o'clock in the morning he had reached the village of Tottenham and here entering a cowshed he went to sleep on the earth floor for three hours. He woke at dawn in great pain, for his ankles, still encircled by the heavy iron collars in which he had escaped, were cut and bruised and swollen. Once more he tried to escape from these fetters, but he could not get them off by himself and now that it was light he knew that the

search for him would be on and that it would be dangerous for him to leave the shelter of his cowshed for help.
Fortunately at seven o'clock it began to rain and all day
long the rain poured heavily down.

From time to time Jack looked out gratefully at the
driving rain and the water-logged fields. Anxious as he
knew his jailers would be to recapture him, they would
not find it easy to organize search parties in that weather.
It was a comfort of a sort. He waited alone for nightfall,
hungry and in pain.

CHAPTER TWELVE

THE LAST DAYS OF FREEDOM

———

BY THE afternoon the news of Jack Sheppard's escape was all over London. There was little other talk either in the polite society of the clubs and coffee houses or in the gin shops and alehouses east of Leicester Fields. *The Daily Post* had published an advertisement similar to that published on September 4th: "Jack Sheppard did brake out of Newgate in the night between the 15th and 16th of this instant of October with double irons on his legs and handcuffs on his hands, with a bright Horse-lock under his other irons.* He is about twenty-two years old, about five Feet four Inches high, very slender of a pale complection, has an impedi-

---

*The advertisement for some reason describes the irons Sheppard wore in Newgate before his escape. It would obviously have been quite impossible for him to have got out of the prison in the way he did, so heavily fettered and handcuffed.

ment or hesitation in his speech, and did wear a Butcher's
Blue Smock with a great coat over it and is a carpenter
or House Joyner by Trade. Whoever will discover or
apprehend him, so that he be brought to justice, shall
have twenty guineas reward to be paid by the Keeper of
Newgate. N.B. If any person conceal him from justice
(knowingly) since he has made his escape it is a felony
and they will be prosecuted for the same."

Similar announcements appeared in all the other papers
and already the ballad writers were busy and the singers
began to celebrate his achievement in the streets. Crowds
of people collected outside the prison and many of them
paid a fee to see the damage done to it.

At eight o'clock that morning William Austin had
entered the cell to look in horrified amazement at the
open handcuffs and padlock and the "cartload" of rubble
on the floor. After a moment's stupefied immobility he
rushed down to the Lodge, where apparently he was at
first so astounded that he could not speak and had to be
revived with a cup of gin before he could gasp out to his
colleagues the extraordinary thing that he had seen.

Austin's colleagues hurried up to the cell to see for
themselves this remarkable sight. One of them said that
Jack must still be in the Red Room above, for that cell
had not been entered for seven years, but another who
had been upstairs to investigate that possibility came
down to report that the door into the Red Room was
lying wide open. Together the jailers followed the trail

of broken doors until they came out onto the roof and saw that in spite of everything which they had done to hold him Jack Sheppard had undoubtedly escaped again.

It was at first supposed that Jack must have had an accomplice inside the prison who had helped him to escape. No one, it was thought, not even Sheppard, could break through those stout doors unaided. The Sheriff came to the prison to make an investigation and the Lord Mayor and the Recorder carried out their own investigation in the Sessions House, where the prison officials were examined meticulously. It was at length reluctantly concluded that no one was to blame and that Sheppard was a very exceptional character who, when sooner or later he was brought back to Newgate, would have to be watched day and night.

But Jack, who lay dozing in the cowshed, was determined that he shouldn't be brought back to Newgate at all. When it was dark he walked into the small village of Tottenham, the fetters round his ankles hidden by the long greatcoat mentioned in *The Daily Post*'s advertisement, and with rather more than two guineas in his pocket. He found a grocer's shop kept by an old woman who was fortunately blind and there he bought some bread and cheese and beer. He asked the old woman if she had a hammer which she could sell him, but she said that she had not. So he trudged painfully back to the cowhouse down the muddy lane. His hunger satisfied, he slept all night. The following day was a Saturday and although he kept a look-out at the cowhouse door he saw no one the whole day. Before dark he had managed to beat one of his irons into the shape of a hoop but try as he might he could not squeeze his foot through it.

It was not until Sunday that the owner of the shed appeared. It was in the afternoon that he came and Jack was asleep so that the man caught him unawares with his legs stretched out and the irons in view beneath the bottom of his coat. "For God's sake," the man asked him nervously, "who are you?" Jack replied quickly: "An unfortunate young man who has been sent to Bridewell about a bastard child as not being able to give security to the Parish and have made my escape."*

"If that's the case," the man said, "it is a small fault indeed for I have formerly been guilty of the same thing myself. However," he added seeing Jack's glittering eyes and white unshaven face, "I do not like your looks and care not how soon you are gone."

Towards evening Jack watching again at the door of the shed saw another man walking by alone. Jack noticed that he was a working man and thought for a moment

*The father of a bastard child was required to maintain it until it was old enough to be apprenticed. The weekly payment, usually half a crown, could be commuted into a lump sum of ten pounds on the payment of which the overseers of the parish would undertake to look after the child and release the father from his weekly obligation. As the child was not expected to live long in the care of a drunken parish nurse or at a workhouse school the money was usually spent by the overseers on a Bacchanalian party called "saddling the spit."

that he might be in the same trade as himself. He decided in any case that it would be safe to speak to him and calling him over he told him the same story that he had told to the owner of the shed and offered him a pound if he would get a smith's hammer and a punch. The man seemed friendly and said that he was a shoemaker and that he would be able to borrow the tools from his neighbour who was a blacksmith.

In a little while the shoemaker returned and he set to work. By five o'clock Jack was free of his irons. He thanked the shoemaker, gave him the pound that he had promised him and told him he could keep the fetters as a memento. Then he put on his stockings and boots and set off for London.

He arrived in London that night disguised as a beggar and coming to a public cellar in Charing Cross he went down and ordered himself a plateful of roast veal. In the cellar "about a dozen people were all talking about Sheppard, and nothing else was talked of" while he was there. The following day, still in the disguise which in his already unshaven, dirty, and dishevelled condition, it was not difficult for him to adopt, he went to a small and little-frequented alehouse in Rupert Street, Piccadilly, where the woman of the house, not recognizing him, spoke to him for a long time about Sheppard and "wished a curse might fall on those who should betray him." Feeling as safe there as he could hope to feel anywhere in the capital he stayed in the alehouse until evening, when he wandered out into the streets and made his way towards Haymarket. There he saw a large crowd which had collected about two ballad singers and walking up to it he mixed with the people to listen to the tales of his own exploits with which the singers were entertaining them. "The Company," Jack afterwards said, "was very merry about the matter."

Everywhere he went the people were talking about him, and a new Jack Sheppard ballad was sung in the streets each night. His mother was reported to have been to St. James's Palace to petition the King for his pardon. Spurious letters alleged to have been written by him were published in the newspapers in the familiar and quasi-literary style of Grub Street. The best and least pretentious of these letters was published in *The British Gazette* of 31st October and was addressed to "Dr. John Ketch* at the sign of the Three-Legg'd Stool near Hyde Park Corner."

*The original Jack Ketch died in 1686. He became famous as a public hangman for his clumsy executions of Lord William Russell in 1683 and of the Duke of Monmouth in 1685 and it was his hopeless inefficiency on these and other occasions which resulted in his name being passed on as a nickname to all subsequent holders of his unpleasant office. Macaulay gave a graphic description of his bungling execution of the Duke of Monmouth. "The first blow," he wrote, "inflicted only a slight wound. The Duke struggled, rose from the block, and looked reproachfully at the executioner. The head sank down once more. The stroke was repeated again and again, but still the neck was not severed, and the body continued to move. Yells of rage and horror rose from the crowd. Ketch flung down the axe with a curse.... 'Fling him over the

Dear Doctor [it began],

After excusing myself to the Reverend Ordinary, my good Friends the Keepers, and Mr. Jonathan Wild, I ought to make some Apology to you, for my withdrawing in so clandestine a Manner, and declining to put myself into your Hands. . . You know that a Dog that has been hang'd on a Crabb-tree, can never love Verjuice; and to tell you the Truth, I have seen some of my Friends under your Hands, make such wry Mouths, and awkward Wrigglings, as have put me out of Conceit with the Operation, and bred in me an Opinion, that (however expert you may be in the *Cito* and *Tuto*) you have not attain'd to the *Jucunde* of your Art. Moreover, I have a mortal Aversion to *Hemp*, it being, as I am inform'd, an Herb of a suffocating Quality; and to deal plain with you, I had rather take a Swing in ten Fathom of Blanket, and venture my Neck four Stories high, than be suspended in ten Foot of Cord, like a Meteor in the Air, to be gazed at by every Fool that thinks it worth his while to make an Holiday. I hate hanging in Suspense for an Hour together: To this I add, that I have naturally an Impediment in my Speech, and should it so happen, (as I know it has to many) that I should entirely lose that Faculty in the Operation, I doubt whether it be in your Power, or that of the whole College, to recover it. . . .

Give my Service to poor Jo. Blueskin: I am told he takes in great Dudgeon my withdrawing in such a Manner; complains

---

rails,' roared the mob. At length the axe was taken up. Two more blows extinguished the last remains of life; but a knife was used to separate the head from the shoulders. The crowd was brought to such an ecstasy of rage that the executioner was in danger of being torn to pieces and was carried away under a strong Guard."

of breach of Articles, by which (as he says) we were oblig'd to *hang together*. I am sorry he is out of Humour; but pray tell him he might have learn'd from a greater Man in the Trade than ever he or I were, to distinguish between the *Spirit* and *Letter* of a Treaty: I defy him to say I ever flinch'd from him in any felonious Attempt we undertook in Company, or that ever I perform'd my Work by *Halves*, as he has lately done. . . . After all, I wish him a safe Deliverance, and if that cannot be, a good Journey. And now, Sir, before I conclude, let me conjure you not to harbour any ill Thought of me from what has happen'd, for 'tis very possible I may perhaps, when you least expect it, convince you and all the World, that I am,

Yours etc.

John Sheppard.

He was reported as having been seen everywhere. *The Daily Journal* said that "the Keepers of Newgate have receiv'd certain Information, that the famous John Sheppard came a few nights ago to the Brewhouse of Messieurs Nichols and Tate in Thames Street, and begged some Wort of the Stoker, which was given him, and that before the proper Officer could be got to secure him, he went off." *Parker's London News* reported that he had been taken in Canterbury, "his habit chang'd into that of a sailor." Another newspaper confirmed a rumour that he had been captured in Reading. Whenever a robbery was committed in London Sheppard was as likely as not to be accused of it. On 31st October *The London Journal* gave an account of a robbery at a "Salesman's Shop in Monmouth Street. It seems the Shop was shut up, and there was only a Hatch fixed at the Door, which the Thief gently open'd without being perceived (there being then Customers in the Shop) and reaching behind the counter, he took his arms full of Cloaths; the Master then saw him and ran to seize him, but only got hold of a Nightgown which he drew from the bundle, whilst the nimble Sharper jump'd over the Hatch and made off with his Booty. . . . The description the man gives of the Person who robbed him, squares exactly with that of the dextrous Sheppard, who is generally believed to be in London playing his old Game."

But although he was apparently seen and recognized every day, and although several arrests were made of young men who resembled him, the real Jack Sheppard remained at liberty.

During the next few days as he wandered from gin shop to alehouse and from doss-house to cellar, he began to feel with justification that he was the most famous man in London, and, with the poor people anyway, the most popular.

Within ten days he was tired of his wanderings, of his filthy clothes and unwashed body. He was tired of being always on the alert, ready to run at a moment's notice. He had heard often enough that he was a hero, but he wanted to look like one and to feel like one. He had moreover no money left.

One day as he walked down Drury Lane he saw in the window of a pawnbroker's shop a suit of fine clothes which

looked about his size. He gazed at the clothes longingly.
He was determined to have them. He judged that the
shop would not be a difficult crib to crack and on the night
of 29th October he broke into it.

The noise he made as he collected together the clothes
that he had set his heart on awakened the two timid
Rawlins brothers in the back room. Jack heard them
whispering nervously together in bed through the partly
open door and walking up to the door he shouted orders
to his imaginary accomplice to shoot the first head that
showed itself. The whispering suddenly ceased and Jack
carried on with his work undisturbed. He escaped from
the house with not only the fashionable suit "of black
Cloth Cloaths" and ruffled shirt but a silver-hilted sword,
a gold watch, a diamond ring, two perriwigs, and two
tortoiseshell snuff-boxes.

The next day, as if the fine clothes had driven all sense
and caution out of him, he strolled importantly about the
town as a man of fashion.

Feeling that he was now sufficiently presentable to
meet his mother again he sent a message to her asking
her to come and see him at the attic room he had by this
time rented in Newport Market.* When she came she

---

*According to *Parker's London News* Sheppard had written a letter
to his mother a few days earlier. The newspaper editor did not explain
how the letter came into his hand, but it is more likely to be genuine
than any other of the letters which were at the time published in his
name."The following letter," the newspaper claimed."being Genuine

burst into tears and throwing herself on her knees at his feet implored him to leave the country immediately before he was caught again. More perhaps in his anxiety to soothe and console his mother, whom he undoubtedly loved, than with any real intention of complying he promised to do as she wished. Comforted by his assurance she became calmer and they sat talking together over a quartern of brandy. When she got up to go he kissed her tenderly and she left him reminding him of his promise.

For the moment, however, he was too excited by his new-found wealth to leave the town where he could enjoy it, particularly as a girl named Kate Cook and a

---

and transcribed from the Original, written by John Sheppard to his Mother, since his Escape, now in her hands, may be depended upon for Truth.

'My dear loving Mother,

'This with my Duty to you, hoping these few lines will find you in good Health, as I am at this present Writing, and this is to let you know, That in my Attempt to make my Escape from the Castle of Newgate, I have had the good Fortune, by the Assistance of God, to make it successful, and to save my Life; and I hope, that by the Grace of God, I shall keep myself from any more of those heinous Crimes, which I have lately committed, and from the Hands of my Enemies. Dear Mother, cast not yourself down, but be of good Heart, for I Hope to be as much Comfort to you as ever I have been the Occasion of Grief. You may let Mr. Applebee, the Printer by Fleet-Ditch know, that I give Orders for you to receive, since I cannot come for it myself, the 8d. a day, which he agreed to allow me during Life, for my *Memorandums*, which will be a good support to you. I would fain let you know where I am, but dare not, for fear of miscarriage. So no more at present, but I rest your loving, dutiful, misfortunate Son,

John Sheppard.' "

friend of hers, Catherine Keys, had just come to live with him in a carefree *ménage à trois* at Newport Market.†
Before leaving the country, if indeed he ever intended to do so, he was determined to have one last fling. With money in his pocket and with two girls to help him spend it he decided to pass the next few days living as recklessly

†Edgworth Bess was still in prison for her part in her lover's escape from the Condemned Hold and was not released until three months later. In the *Daily Journal* of 11th September Sheppard was reported to have said that she was the "cause of all his Misfortunes and Misery." It is more likely that this was Parson Wagstaff's opinion given to the journalist as being Sheppard's. Jack and Bess appear to have been devoted to one another and he was unlikely to have borne her a grudge for having betrayed him when she fell into the hands of Wild. He had reason to know the sort of treatment she feared and might well have received. Jack was not, in spite of what Wagstaff subsequently intimated, a man who regretted his wild life, except in so far as it had shamed and saddened his mother, or who was likely to have spoken ill of a woman who loved him and who had done so much to help him in the past.

Over a year later Edgworth Bess was transported for the theft of six silver teaspoons. A dram-shop keeper who was a witness at her trial deposed that while drinking with her accomplice, John Smith, she pulled out the spoons, "kist 'em and said, 'These were left me by my Dear John Sheppard, and I have just now fetched 'em out of pawn from Mrs. Pocock's.' "

Kate Cook and Catherine Keys seemed also, as indeed did all his companions, to have afterwards remembered him with affection. At the trial of Cook and Keys on 4th December (on charges of assisting Sheppard in the Rawlins robbery and of receiving the stolen goods; charges of which they were both acquitted) more than one witness testified that Kate Cook had spoken of Sheppard with love and admiration. Mr. Crowder, the owner of the Dolphin alehouse, to which some of the stolen goods were alleged to have been taken, swore that Cook had boasted to him, in a frankly lascivious moment, that she had been Jack's washerwoman, "for she had often wash'd his——betwixt her——."

and dissolutely as he thought might be expected of the remarkable hero he had discovered himself to be.

It could only be a matter of days now before he was caught. He seemed indeed to be inviting capture.

One day after having had a meal with Kate and Catherine at a tavern in Newgate Street, he ordered a hackney coach and, no doubt far from sober, drove along the walls of the prison and through the arch of the gateway and past the entrance door to the Lodge.

The following day he was even more incautious. After drinking in a tavern in Maypole Street, Clare Market, he met Moll Frisky, a former mistress of his, and together they went from tavern to tavern getting more and more drunk. He was recognized, probably not for the first time that day, outside a butcher's shop in Drury Lane just before midnight, and later on he was recognized again as he sat drinking with Moll Frisky in Mrs. Campbell's dram shop. The potboy of the Rose and Crown opposite, who saw him when he came into Mrs. Campbell's "to ask for Pots," told his master the tavern-keeper that he thought that the man drinking in the dram shop over the way was Jack Sheppard.

The tavern-keeper was unfortunately the Head Borough of the district and could not afford to ignore the boy's excitement. He sent for Mr. Eyles, a constable, who had no difficulty in arresting the by now incapable Jack, "in his handsome suit of black Cloaths and light Tye Perriwig," and bundling him shouting drunkenly for help into a coach. Jack's senses, as he afterwards explained to Defoe, were "at length quite overcome with the quantities and variety of liquor I had all the day been drinking of . . . and when apprehended I do protest I was altogether incapable of resisting and scarce knew what they were doing to me."

All the way back to Newgate Jack shouted, "Murder, help for God's sake, Rogues, I am murder'd and am in the Hands of Bloodhounds, help for Christ's sake." But the hackney coach, which was driven quickly, passed by "the several thousands of people assembled in Holborn" who could do nothing to help him.

James Figg

from a painting by J. Ellys,
engraved by R. Grave

Jonathan Wild

from a contemporary print,
engraved by T. Cook

Daniel Defoe

from an engraving by
H. Barrett

Jack Sheppard

from a sketch by
Sir James Thornhill

The Execution of the Idle Apprentice

from the engraving by Hogarth

CHAPTER THIRTEEN

THE SECOND TRIAL

—

O N FRIDAY, 6th November, the Duke of Newcastle, the Secretary of State for the Southern
Department, wrote a letter to Sir Philip Yorke,
the Attorney General:

Whitehall Nov. 6 1724

Sir—His Majesty being informed of the extraordinary escapes
that John Sheppard a felon convict has twice made out of Newgate and how very dangerous a person he is, has commanded
me to signify to you his pleasure that you do *forthwith* cause
him, in the proper course of law, to be brought before the
Court of King's Bench to the end that execution may *without
delay* be awarded against him: and that he may be the more
securely kept his Majesty would have you move the Court
that he may be remanded to Newgate to remain in custody
there until his execution.

I am, Sir,

Your most humble servant,

Holles Newcastle.*

*British Museum. Addl. MSS. 36, 135, fo. 87.

Four days later at half-past ten in the morning a coach drew up outside the gate of the Lodge and Jack hand-cuffed and in fetters was driven away to Westminster Hall closely guarded. The news of his appearance that day in the Court of King's Bench had spread quickly and by the time the coach reached Temple Bar large crowds were already lining the route. Outside Westminster Hall a mass of people shouted and pushed and jostled each other in an attempt to catch sight of the great prison-breaker. But he was hustled quickly out of the coach and few people saw him.

Once inside his handcuffs and fetters were knocked off and he was taken into the courtroom.

The Court, having heard the report of the conviction at the Old Bailey Sessions, required little more than evidence of identification. This was provided by the Keeper of Newgate and his assistant, who both swore that he was the same man against whom sentence of death had already been pronounced by the Recorder. The rest of the proceedings were formalities. Jack made a speech in his own defence which was not so much a denial or an excuse as a restrained plea for mercy and when it was over and Jack's petition to the King had been read to the Court there was little else to do. Jack was asked more out of interest than for any other reason why after having escaped from prison and having the opportunity to get out of the country he should have committed further

crimes and allowed himself to be retaken. He replied that
he was out of money and had no other way of earning his
living and that he had intended to leave the country on
the Monday following his recapture.

Before formally sentencing him to death the President
of the Court told Jack that if he would give any information which resulted in the arrest of an accomplice he might
be treated with leniency but that this betrayal of his
abettors was the only way in which he could escape the
full rigours of the law.

Jack's confident reply to this offer was immediate and
apparently sincere. His only assistant, he said, with a
touch of pride was "God Almighty." For a moment there
was a shocked silence in the courtroom and then the
President hastily reprimanded him for his profanity. Not
in the least put out by the President's words or the cold
looks of the other members of the Court, Jack went on to
say that if they would get someone to put his handcuffs
on again he would be pleased to show them how he
needed no accomplices to get them off. The members of
the Court looked at him in amazement, wondering what
on earth the fellow was going to say next. Without
further questions the President delivered his severe
speech of reproof and admonition and sentenced him to
death.

Before he was allowed to leave Westminster Hall he
had to keep an appointment with the Earl of Macclesfield,

the Lord Chancellor, who had heard that Jack Sheppard's case was being heard that morning and had expressed a desire to meet the famous young man.

The Lord Chancellor was the husband of the Lady Macclesfield whose illegitimate son, Richard Savage, was to be tried for murder in 1727. He was a peculiarly unfortunate man. Having lost a considerable sum of money in the South Sea Bubble speculations he thought that he would be able to improve his finances when he was appointed to the Lord Chancellorship. The salary was £4,000 a year free of tax and he was paid £14,000 as a capital sum when he took up his appointment. Furthermore he knew that the profits from the sale of Masterships in Chancery had for long been a recognized perquisite of the office. But no other Lord Chancellor charged as much as he did. He put up the prices to such an extent that the Masters to reimburse themselves fell to misappropriating the funds lodged in the Chancery Court. It was alleged by the prosecution at his trial in the House of Lords that he had dipped into Court funds himself. He was found guilty and declared unfit ever to hold again an office under the Crown. His fine of £30,000 he paid within a few weeks, knowing that the King, who was a personal friend of his was very upset by the indignities he had suffered and had promised to recompense him by instalments. After paying the first instalment the King died.

As a rich man impoverished, a disgraced friend of the King, and a cuckold, he was a favourite subject for ballad writers. "The Epistle from Jack Sheppard to The Late Lord Chancellor of England" is a good example of the scandalous style of the contemporary ballad.

Since your Curiosity led you so far
As to send for me to the Chancery Bar,
To show what a couple of Rascals we are,
    Which no Body can deny.

Were your virtues and mine to be weighed in a Scale,
I fear, honest Tom, that thine would prevail,
  For you broke through all laws while I only broke jail,
    Which no Body can deny.

Yet something I hope to my merit is due,
Since there ne'er was so barefaced a Bungler as you,
And that I'm the more dext'rous rogue of the two,
    Which no Body can deny.

We, who rob for a living, if taken, must die;
Those who plunder poor Orphans pray answer me why
They deserve not a rope more than Blueskin and I,
    Which no Body can deny.

Tho' the Masters were Rascals, that you should swing for't
Would be damnable hard, for your Lordship, in short,
Was no more than the Jonathan Wild of the Court,
    Which no Body can deny.

Excuse me the Freedom in writing to thee,
For the World then allow'd they never did see
A Pair so well match'd as your Lordship and Me.

At thy present Disgrace, my Lord, never repine,
For Fame rings of Nothing but thy Tricks and mine,
And our Names will alike in all History shine,
     Which no Body can deny.

The interview with Macclesfield over, Jack was
escorted to the Hall gate. Outside in the street the numbers of the crowd had enormously increased, and as Jack
appeared the onlookers, "the most numerous crowds of
People that ever was seen in London," surged forward
shouting and trampling over the bodies of those who
stumbled and fell. Several people were seriously injured
and a constable who tried to hold back the pushing crowd
broke his leg in the attempt. But Jack, closely guarded by
a strong contingent of jailers, was taken safely into the
waiting coach and carried back to his cell.

Jack was more than normally uncomfortable there.
His jailers, anxious to ensure that he had not the least
chance of escaping again, manacled him more elaborately
than they would have thought necessary for a powerful
and ferocious animal. The weight of his irons was said
at the time to have been three hundred pounds, which
was probably more than twice the weight of his own body.
Before his trial he had been kept like this in the foul and
fetid atmosphere, every muscle cramped and every limb
in agonized discomfort, for nearly a fortnight. Watched
day and night in the light of a guttering candle by a
succession of warders who dared not grant him the
privileges usually accorded to a prisoner of his distinction

and popularity for fear that he might escape, he had laid on the stone floor uncomplaining and cheerful, talking as gaily as if he were enjoying a glass of brandy at The Black Lion. Day after day curious people had paid their entrance fee to come to see him. It now cost a well-dressed man, holding a handkerchief soaked in vinegar up to his powdered nose, no less than four shillings and by the end of the first week more than a thousand people had paid to see him.

"Nothing," a journalist had written on 7th November, "contributes so much to the entertainment of the town at present as the adventures of the famous housebreaker and gaolbreaker John Sheppard. 'Tis thought the Keepers of Newgate have got 200*l.* already by the crowds of people who flock daily to Sheppard." Country people too had come up to London specially to see one or other of the "three great Curiosities as this Town at present affords viz.: The two young Lyons stuff'd at the Tower; the Ostrich on Ludgate-Hill; and the famous John Sheppard in Newgate."

As soon as he returned from Westminster Hall Jack was clamped up again in his fetters and manacles in his dark and dismal cell.

But the following day he was brought back into the Condemned Hold once more. Mr. Pitt thought that so long as Blueskin was there it would be as well to keep his young friend Sheppard out of it, but Blueskin earlier on that morning had begun his journey to Tyburn* and Jack's only companion in the Hold was Lewis Houssart, a barber of French extraction condemned to death for the murder of his wife. Jack learned from his companion and from the turnkeys the strange and horrible story of the little barber.

He had, it appeared, after three years' marriage, "left his wife in disgust" and moving to another district passed himself off as a bachelor. Some time later he met a widow who attracted him and he married her. His new wife, hearing a rumour that he was already married, accused him of having married her bigamously. He strenuously denied that this was so, offered to take the sacrament upon it and reassured her saying that "in a little time I will make you sensible I have no other wife." He soon took steps to prove it. Visiting his former wife he found her ill in bed and returned the following day with "medicine which had the appearance of conserve of roses, which threw her into such severe convulsive fits that her life was despaired of for some hours; but at length she recovered."

Thinking that he had better kill her by more direct and positive means he dressed himself up a few days later as a gentleman in a white coat and with a sword and cane,

---

*In his passage to Tyburn Blueskin call'd at the Griffin Tavern in Holborn, where he drank and shew'd much Insolence and ill Behaviour; and when he came to the Gallows, was so drunk as to reel and faulter in his Speech—*Parker's London News.*

and went to the street in which his wife now lived with her mother. He found a boy in the street to whom he gave a penny to go up and tell his mother-in-law that a gentleman wished to speak to her in a nearby tavern. Waiting until the woman came out of the house he then went in himself and cut his wife's throat with a razor. "Thus murdered she was found by her mother on her return."

Houssart was immediately arrested, but at his trial the boy was too frightened to come forward with his evidence and he was acquitted. While still detained in Newgate on the bigamy charge, the boy was persuaded that he would not, as he feared, be hanged as an accessory and decided to give evidence after all. Houssart was brought to trial for the second time and the boy's clear evidence that he recognized the prisoner as the man in the white coat who had given him the penny made the case look black for the accused. He could not be mistaken, the boy said plainly, because the prisoner had stood under the light of a lantern outside a butcher's shop and he saw his face quite distinctly. Another witness for the prosecution said that Houssart had offered him twenty guineas if he would swear that he had been drinking with him in Newgate Street on the night of the murder. Houssart, faced by this damning evidence, admitted that he did give the boy a penny to get the old woman out of the house, but that he had gone in with the intention only of giving his wife "a touch with the razor, but did not think of killing her."

He was found guilty and sentenced to death and now waited with Jack in the Condemned Hold to be called out into the hanging cart.

The Condemned Hold had been much altered since Jack had shown how easy it was for him to escape from it. The space through which Jack had squeezed in his mistress's nightdress had now been boarded up. New and harsher rules for the prisoners' conduct had been made. They were no longer permitted to come up to the barrier to talk to visitors. Jack in any case, weighted down by his irons and stapled to the floor, could not have done so.

But the visitors could and did still flock into the Hold to see him. Jack asked the more influential-looking amongst this "abundance of gentry and nobility" to intercede with the King on his behalf. The King's interest in the young felon, however, was purely objective. His curiosity there is no reason to believe was in any way tinged with pity.

One visitor who took an instant liking to Jack was James Figg, the famous prizefighter whose rough and battered features were made familiar to his contemporaries by his friend Hogarth. Figg, with the black patches on his head covering his several scars, was a well-known character in the London of his day. Every year he was in attendance at his celebrated booth on the Bowling Green at Southwark during the time of Southwark Fair and he kept an academy in Oxford Road where gentlemen might learn how to defend themselves against the attacks of ruffians and street robbers. His business card designed by Hogarth advertised his ability:

James Figg,
Master of ye Noble Science of Defence
On ye right hand in Oxford Road
near Adam and Eve Court teaches Gentle-
men ye use of ye small back sword &
Quarterstaff at home and abroad.

He had a large following and a distinguished clientele. He boasted once to a friend that he had not bought a shirt in years, as each time he went into his amphitheatre to demonstrate his skill with the broadsword he would send round to all his rich young students for a shirt. They, eager to please their master, would immediately send him one of their best. After the fight they saw the shirt cut and dirty and stained and each one, presuming it to be the one which he had lent, did not think it worth while to ask for it back.

He confessed to being very taken with Jack and made him promise that on his ride to Tyburn he would stop at his Academy in the Oxford Road to drink a toast with him.

Another and more distinguished visitor was Sir James Thornhill, whose work was so greatly admired by the young Hogarth. Thornhill, who was Serjeant-Painter to the Crown, had collaborated with Wren on the decorations to the dome of the new St. Paul's and the Painted Hall of Greenwich Palace, and it is today as a painter of highly imaginative frescoes that he is chiefly remembered.

There was, however, in 1724 no more fashionable or better-known portraitist. Kneller had just died and Reynolds was still a child, while Hogarth, his future son-in-law, had scarcely begun to demonstrate his formidable talent. His position as Serjeant-Painter was secure and there was no one, it was thought, better qualified to portray the sad and intelligent features of the famous little thief.

The portrait shows him sitting at a table under the barred window of the Hold, his legs crossed, his wrists handcuffed resting on the table. There is an expression in the eyes of infinite sadness and regret, but the mouth, although pathetic in repose, is sensual and humorous. It is a face not far from tears nor yet far from laughter.

This atmosphere of chiaroscuro and unexpected changes of mood is apparent also in the two accounts of Sheppard's life and adventures which Defoe was writing at this time for Mr. Applebee, the printer in Blackfriars. Daniel Defoe, when he visited Jack and obtained from him the first-hand accounts which make his narratives so evocative and convincing, was an ageing man. Twenty years before he had been described as a "middle-aged, spare man, of a brown complexion, and dark brown coloured hair, but wears a wig, a sharp chin, grey eyes and a large mole near his mouth." He was now about sixty-four and before taking to journalism as a full-time occupation he had been a soldier, a businessman, and a secret agent. The experience of a man of the world and the observant eye of an artist gave to his writings their distinctive flavour of irony, sensibility, and truth, and their bright flashes of revealing detail. When he came to talk to Jack in Newgate he came as a man who had been imprisoned himself, who had been bankrupt and wronged and misunderstood and lonely. He came as a writer who was interested in the man of action rather than in the man of ideas. He was concerned only with those who had lived hard. No contemporary journalist could have understood Jack Sheppard better.

The persistent and ever-questioning Rev. Mr. Wagstaff and his fellow chaplains from other prisons were less sympathetic. They had little concern for his immortal soul and spent their time in his company mainly in the hope that they would hear a new titbit which would provide good copy for their forthcoming pamphlets.*

*Wagstaff was an experienced writer of sensational "Last Dying Confessions" and his pamphlets were printed and published by John Applebee, Defoe's publisher. In *The Daily Journal* of 15th and 16th September an advertisement appeared apparently having been written by Sheppard but more likely having been inserted by Wagstaff without his knowledge. The advertisement ran: "The Time of my Dissolution approaching, and in all probability after my Decease, false accounts of my evil Life and Conversation, etc. will be publish'd by some designing Persons for the Lucre of Gain and Profit; I have therefore for the satisfaction of the World, communicated my whole Life and wicked Actions to the Reverend Mr. Wagstaff, in order to be made Publick, to the End all other young Persons may be warn'd from following the like Courses, by my sad and dreadful Example.

In the chapel of Newgate   witness my Hand
   this 14th of September 1724   John Sheppard"

Jack became understandably impatient with these gossiping hypocrites and once furiously turned on them and declared that one good file would be of more use to him than all the Bibles in the world.

It was a rare outburst. Most of the time he was pleasant, cheerful, and friendly to everyone who came to see him. It seems that even in his present apparently hopeless situation, handcuffed and fettered and stapled to the floor, watched day and night, guarded more carefully than any prisoner in Newgate had ever been guarded before, he never lost hope of making his last dramatic escape to freedom. As the day of his execution approached he realized that to escape from the prison would be impossible, but once out of the prison during the long march to Tyburn he felt sure his opportunity would come. A friend had been able to smuggle in to him a sharp knife which on the night before his execution he was determined to fix behind the buttons of his waistcoat if he got an opportunity of doing so. It was usual for the irons of a condemned felon to be removed on the last morning and for his wrists to be bound with cord. Jack hoped by leaning forward in the cart and forcing the blade of the knife against the cord he would be able to cut it and once free throw himself into the dense crowd as the Tyburn procession passed through Little Turnstile, a narrow passage near Lincoln's Inn Fields. And even if this plan failed and he got as far as the gallows he still had a chance.

He had already made arrangements with his friends to

rent a room close to Tyburn and to employ the services of a surgeon who, as soon as the body of Jack was brought to him, would use his skill to bring it back to consciousness. There were precedents enough, Jack knew, for his resuscitation.

For death by hanging to be instantaneous as it is today was then extremely rare. The condemned man hung for minutes at the end of the rope struggling for breath and died by slow strangulation. If he was cut down while unconscious, but before death came to him, there was always a good chance that he could be revived. Even after being hanged for twenty minutes or more men had been known to be resuscitated. The famous surgeon Sir William Petty had added to his celebrity by reviving an apparent corpse at an anatomical lecture. Seeing signs of life in the female body which had been brought to him for dissection he bled it thoroughly, put it to bed next to another woman, and forced restoratives through its stretched lips. The woman recovered and the students clubbed together to buy her a present. Subsequently she married and lived happily for fifteen years until she died peacefully in bed. A less happy story is told of John Hunter, who brought back life into a body which had been brought to him for dissection. The man on being revived looked to Hunter for his support and called on him from time to time for a loan, telling him that as he had been brought back to a life which he ought by rights to have left, Hunter ought to feel responsible for his maintenance. Hunter evidently fulfilled what he thought were his moral obligations until one day as he was about to begin another dissection he recognized the body of the persistent blackmailer under his knife. He did not, it is to be supposed, repeat the former successful operation on the corpse's windpipe.

The case of Half-hang'd Smith was one with which Jack was almost certain to be familiar. Smith's reprieve came just after the hanging had begun. He was cut down and immediately operated on. He afterwards described in vivid detail the great pain as the cart drove away letting the weight of his body wrench against his neck and as his "spirits" forced themselves out of his eye-sockets in a sudden flash of light. The pain as he was revived made him wish "those hanged who cut him down." But he survived.

So Jack kept up his spirits with these stories of resuscitation and trusted to his friends to cut his body down, wrap it up in hot blankets, and get it to the surgeon without too much delay.

Sunday, 15th November, was his last day in the prison. During the morning he was taken up to the chapel for the special service which was held the day before an execution and was led into the condemned pew as hundreds of curious spectators jostled each other to catch a glimpse of him. The chapel was open to the public on these occasions and the congregation, boisterous and profane, was with difficulty silenced to listen to the condemned sermon, which although intended to comfort the capital convicts more often than not reduced them to the most abject depression and terrified apprehension.

The spiritual welfare of the condemned man was further provided for in the will of a generous citizen, Robert Dow, who had bequeathed an annuity to the churchwardens of St. Sepulchre's on condition that on the midnight preceding an execution they arranged for the bellman to toll the big bell and for the sexton to visit the window of the Condemned Hold. The sexton was to wake the prisoners with "twelve solemn towles with double strokes" and intone for their comfort and consolation the following strange but simple verse:

> All you that in the Condemned Hold do lie,
> Prepare you, for tomorrow you shall die:
> Watch all and pray; the hour is drawing near
> That you before the Almighty must appear:
> Examine well yourselves: in time repent;
> That you may not to eternal flames be sent.
> And when St. Sepulchre's bell tomorrow tolls,
> The Lord above have mercy on your souls!

As the mournful voice of the sexton died away Jack knew that Sunday had passed and it was the morning of his execution. In a few hours' time he would be riding through those streets outside to Tyburn.

CHAPTER FOURTEEN

TYBURN FAIR

—

NOT since Claude Duval the highwayman had been hanged more than fifty years before had a hanging aroused such excitement and enthusiasm. Before dawn the spectators came out of their houses into the cold November morning to reserve places for themselves at the best points along the route between the prison and Tyburn. At Tyburn itself the grand-stand seats known by the *aficionados* as Mother Proctor's Pews were already filling up and around the gallows those who could not afford Mother Proctor's prices tramped up and down with hot potatoes in their pockets and mufflers round their necks, determined in spite of the cold and the long wait to be in the front row when the fun started.

It was not until nine o'clock that the hero of the drama was called out of his cell to begin his long performance. Well washed and brushed and wearing the smart black suit, which no one had thought of returning to the Rawlins brothers, his first duty was to attend Holy Communion in the chapel. Then after a late breakfast he was taken to the Press Yard where the Under Sheriff, Mr. Watson, made the customary demand for the condemned man to be handed into his custody, giving, as if he were already dead, a formal receipt for his body. This ceremony over, Jack was handed over to the care of a smith who hammered off his fetters. Jack held out his wrists for the handcuffs to be removed also, but no notice was taken of them. When it became apparent that his handcuffs were to be left on, Jack asked earnestly that they should be removed, saying that it was cruel to deny him the right afforded to every other condemned prisoner and that the indignity of being handcuffed during his last few hours on earth was more than he should be asked to bear. No attention was paid to his pleading and Jack, furious that his carefully prepared plan of escape should be thwarted in this way, lost his temper and struggled furiously with the Knight of the Halter, whose duty it was to bind the gallows rope round the chest of the condemned man. When the Knight of the Halter had at last finished his grotesque task and Jack was a little calmer, Mr. Watson, who believed that Sheppard's fury must be prompted by disappointment rather than loss of pride, came up to search him.

He ran his hands up his legs, tapped the full pockets of his coat and the ruffled shirt. Suddenly he stepped back crying out in pain as the exquisitely sharp knife in Jack's waistcoat cut into his fingers. Jack apologized to Watson as the knife was carefully removed and told his jailers in the most friendly way of his plan to escape into the dense crowds of sympathetic spectators he expected to find waiting to see him at Lincoln's Inn Fields. The jailers laughed as he explained his plan to them in that curiously effective and amusing, hesitant style of his with which they had grown familiar.

As he spoke the City Marshal was forming up the procession in the street outside the Lodge gate. The crowds* had increased by now and the noise was thunderous. Every window was full of shouting excited faces pressing this way and that so as not to miss anything that went on in the street below. Even the roofs of the houses were crowded with people expectantly watching, waving to friends, shouting greetings across the roof-tops. Below them in the cobbled street the packed and swaying heads were numberless. Regularly and mournfully the great deep bell of St. Sepulchre's, which was tolled only when a condemned man was taken to Tyburn, boomed and boomed.

As the prison gate opened a cheer went up from those who saw it, but the cheer was scarcely heard in the general constant roar. Jack stepped up into the cart and the procession with difficulty moved off.

A contingent of peace-officers led the way. Behind them marched the City Marshal, followed by the Under

*An eyewitness estimated the numbers of the crowd, probably without undue exaggeration, at 200,000.

Sheriff and a posse of constables. Then came the cart with the hangman squatting up in front on top of the coffin. Behind the hangman sat the prison chaplain whose duty it was to prepare the condemned man for the life to come and to induce him to repent of his sins while there was still time for repentance. Mr. Wagstaff, however, does not appear to have taken his duty very seriously and during this last hour while he had the convict to himself, hoped to discover some new and worthwhile gossip about his former life or the manner of his death which would be good material for a newspaper article or a pamphlet and thus steal a march on his colleagues.

Following the cart was a troop of soldiers in red coats and tricornes, carrying pikes and adding colour and dignity to the otherwise rather drab and ragged procession. Finally came a second posse of constables on horseback.

The peace-officers, ambling rather than marching, conscious that the crowd saw no glory in their task, brought the parade to a shambling halt opposite the steps leading to the porch of the church of St. Sepulchre.

Here the first ceremony took place. The bellman who the night before had delivered his message outside the window of the Condemned Hold stood with bell in hand behind the church wall and, as the condemned man was drawn up in his cart to the steps of the church, rang his bell in an interval between the deep booms from the belfry above, and intoned this gloomy admonition for the benefit of the bystanders as well as for the comfort of the convict.

All good people pray heartily unto God for this poor sinner who is now going to his death, for whom this great bell doth toll.

You that are condemned to die, repent with lamentable tears; ask mercy of the Lord for the salvation of your own soul, through the merits, death and passion of Jesus Christ, who now sits at the right hand of God, to make intercession for as many as penitently return to Him.

> Lord have mercy upon you
> Christ have mercy upon you
> Lord have mercy upon you
> Christ have mercy upon you.

As soon as the prayer was delivered it was the custom for girls on the church steps to throw nosegays and kisses to the condemned man, who stood up in the cart to receive them. Jack as he stood up smiling at the galaxy of cheering, shouting faces was showered with flowers and ribbons and petals and bits of coloured paper. "His behaviour," a journalist noted the following day in the *London News*, "was modest but his concern seemed less than could be expected from one under such fatal circumstances." It seemed indeed to more than one observer that he was almost enjoying himself. He was constantly alert so as not to miss any opportunity of escape which might present itself and if he had no chance to throw himself amongst a group of friends in the crowd his plans for resuscitation were all carefully laid. He smiled cheerfully to all around him; he nodded politely on occasions to Mr. Wagstaff, who said afterwards that the extraordinary young man had admitted to him that he felt as content as if "he was going to enjoy an estate of £100 a year," and when a friend of his suddenly pushed his way through the crowd and past the line of constables to whisper something in his ear, Jack laughed heartily.

The parade had now passed slowly down Snow Hill and over the Fleet by the narrow stone bridge, up Holborn Hill and past the church of St. Andrew's, where even the roof was covered with people who stared giddily down from behind the narrow safety of the parapet wall onto the dense and rolling mass of heads and shoulders below.

At the sign of The City of Oxford in Oxford Road, Marylebone Fields, where Jack's new friend James Figg had his Academy and Gymnasium, the procession once more was halted at Jack's request. The famous prize-fighter came forward with a tray of drinks and gave Jack a pint of mulled sack which he took in both hands to warm his fingers as he drank. Figg handed drinks to the officials around the cart and to friends and pupils of his who had come to see Jack again or to meet him for the first and last time. Glasses were raised and toasts were drunk while farther down the route the spectators grew impatient at the delay, stamping their feet, blowing on their fingers in the cold, and shouting for the cart to move on again and for the hanging to start.

Warmed by the wine Jack felt in better spirits than ever as the hangman slapped the buttocks of the horse and the slow journey continued. On the right of him now as he was driven down the Oxford Road was the open country of Marylebone Fields and the villages of Hampstead and Highgate on the high ground beyond, and ahead of him just beyond the junction of Oxford Road and Edgware Road and near the wall of Hyde Park he could just see the gaunt foreboding gallows and the tiered seats beside them. As he caught sight of the gallows, so large that they could hold twenty-one hanging bodies at the same time, his courage seemed for a moment to leave him and he appeared for the first time apprehensive and uncertain. He never from now on recovered his former carefree lighthearted insouciance. He became serious and thoughtful but at the same time dignified and courteous and, after the first sickening sight of the immense and ugly gallows, he recovered his courage and certainty of movement.

Nearly half of the page is devoted to "John Sheppard's last Epistle." For three months Sheppard had been front-page news in all London newspapers, not a week passing without some mention of him. *The Daily Journal* wrote on 18th November "Nothing more at present is talked on about Town, than Jack Sheppard," and *Parker's London News* on that day devoted the whole of one of its six pages to him. On 4th November it reported that "his Majesty has been pleased to send for the two prints of Sheppard shewing the manner of his being chained to the floor in the Castle at Newgate."

The Daily Journal.

MONDAY NOVEMBER 16. 1724

Lisbon, Oct. 17.

LAST Week, the King went by Water to the Cloifter of St. Jofeph de Ribamar, and regaled the Fryars there with a magnificent Dinner, according to his annual Cuftom: Whence he was no fooner return'd to his Palace, but he found himfelf out of Order with a fore Throat, which obliged him to keep his Chamber four days; but he is now perfectly recover'd. On the 12th inftant, between Two and Three o'Clock in the Morning, we felt here a confiderable Shock of an Earthquake, which frightned the People a little, but did no other Damage.

Frankfort, Nov. 15. 'Tis affirm'd that in cafe of a War, the Emperor will take into his Service a confiderable Number of Troops from divers Princes of the Empire. In Alface, and in the Bifhopricks of Mets, Toul, and Verdun, they are by an Order from Court taking an Account of what Corn is in the Magazines.

Hanover, Nov. 17. Yefterday Morning early, Prince Frederick fet out for Guiflhorn, eight Leagues off, to take the Diverfion of Hunting; and is expected back here to-morrow.

Hamburgh, Nov. 17. They wrote from Copenhagen the 14th inftant, that Mr. Finch, late Envoy of England to the Crown of Sweden, arrived there that day from Stockholm, and fet forward on his Journey towards Fredericksburg, defigning to wait on the King of Denmark before he proceeds for Holland.

London, November 16.

Mr. Du Commin, the King's Meffenger, who arrefted Brigadier Mackintofh and his Brother in the Highlands of Scotland, is recover'd of the Wounds he received in the Tumult which happen'd on that Occafion, and waits till Mr. John Mackintofh is able to travel, in order to bring him to London.

The Conge de Elire being fent down to the Dean and Chapter of York, to elect an Archbifhop of that Province; the Dean and Chapter did on Wednefday laft elect and return the moft Reverend Dr. Lancelot Blackbourn, (Lord Bifhop of Exeter) into that See.

Mr. Bever, Steward to the Earl of Hallifax, fucceeds Henry Seager, Efq· deceafed, as Clerk in the Annuity Office in the Exchequer.

Mr. Sturgis is made Comptroller of the Cuftoms at Hull, in the room of the faid Henry Seager, deceas'd.

JOHN SHEPPARD's laft Epiftle.

I.

TO the *Hundreds* of *Drury* I write,
And to all my Filching Companions,
The *Buttocks* who pad it all Night,
The *Wh--res*, the *Thieves*, and the *Stallions*.
I then who am now in the *Witt*,
Does rattle my *Darby's* with Pleafure,
And laughs at the *Cullies* I've bitt,
For I have ftill Store of their Treafure.

II.

Moll Frisky was here t'other Night,
And *tipp'd* me a Quartern of *Diddle*,
And fwore fhe'd been dam--ble *tight*
Upon *Fitchford* who plays on the *Fiddle*.
She *fnaffled* his *Main*, *Poll* and *T--l*,
For which She was *rubb'd* to the *Witt*, Sir,
And now the *Wh--re pads* it in *Jail*,
And laughs at poor *Fitchford* She bitt, Sir.

III.

This Time I expect to be *Nubb'd*,
My *Dudds* are grown wond'rous *Seedy*;
Pray fend me fome *Peck* and fome *Bub*,
A *Slat* or a *Board* to the Needy.
Pray now do not bring it your felf,
The *Giffing Culls* are at the *Old-Baily*;
I'd rather you fend it by half,
If the *Harman* fhould touch you he'd nail ye.

IV.

'Tis in vain to hope for a *Reprieve*,
The Sheriff's come down with his *Warrant*;
An *Account* I behind me. muft leave
Of my *Birth, Education* and *Parents*.
My *Darby's* knock'd off in the *Witt*,
My Friends to die penitent pray me;
The *Nubbing Cull* pops on the *Cheat*,
And into the *Tumbler* conveys me.

V.

I am ambled from *Witt* to the *Tree*,
As order'd by my fad Sentence,
The *Gownman* he there comes to me,
And talks a long Time of Repentance.
I am up to the *Jagger dubb'd* tight,
Then I loudly muft join in a *Chorus*,
My *Peepers* are hid from the Light,
The *Tumbler* wheels of and I *Morris*.

On Saturday South-Sea Stock was 121. Ditto Annuities 105 and a half. India 153. Bank 131. Ditto Circulation three 4ths per Cent. Prem. African 12 three 8ths. York-Buildings 17. Royal-Exchange Affurance 55 and a half. London Affurance 8 per Share. Welfh Copper 33 s. South-Sea Bonds 1 l. 12 s. Prem. India Bonds 1 l. 19 s.

The front page of *The Daily Journal*, 16th November 1724

(See footnote on opposite page.)

As the cart drew up under the gallows the pigeon which signalled his safe arrival at Tyburn was released and flew back to Newgate, while the constables and soldiers formed a ring round the Fatal Tree to force back the crowd so that the hangman might have sufficient room to perform his duty.

While this was being done and while Mr. Watson, the Under Sheriff, was persuading Jack to confess to the robberies at Mr. Phillips's and Miss Cook's, the rough and tumble fun of Tyburn Fair went on.

As the hanging day was a public holiday for the labouring class and it was not often that the workers could take a Monday morning off like this, they were determined to make the most of it. Hogarth's picture of Tyburn Fair gives a vivid impression of the scene. The central figure in the cart is for the moment forgotten amidst the squabbling and shouting and brawling in the foreground. The gingerbread seller and the seller of the felon's already published "Last Dying Speech and Confession" shout their wares against each other at the tops of their voices. The orange seller is too busy gouging out the eyes of a man who has knocked over her cart to shout anything other than abuse. Above her a group of women in a high cart, where they will get a good view of the hanging, are drinking gin or reaching down to buy another glass from the gin seller on the ground below. A man holds a struggling yapping dog by the tail, standing ready to fling it at the mournful-looking parson in the cart; a group of men fight furiously with sticks and a woman fights with her massive fists, having dropped her baby on the ground to deliver a finishing blow; two boys point and laugh at a soldier who has fallen up to his knees in a pool of mud; a pickpocket takes advantage of the violent commotion to push his cautious hand into a nearby pocket.

Beyond the noisy, bruising, and smelly rabble can be seen the grandstand seats where the more well-to-do sit. For hangings were not a spectacle only to be enjoyed by the vulgar. There were few contemporary men of fashion who did not enjoy a good hanging. Mother Proctor was said to have made £500 when Earl Ferrers was hanged in 1760 for a shooting a servant, and at Duval's hanging in 1670 ladies in masks and in tears came to watch and to throw flowers to their hero who was believed to have seduced more than a few of them. In the years between, George Selwyn, a friend of Walpole, and an elegant man of wit and fashion, admitted that he never missed a hanging if he could help it. Once he went specially to Paris to see Damien broken on the wheel for his attempted assassination of Louis XV and on another occasion excused himself for having attended Lord Lovat's execution by saying that he made amends by going to the undertaker's afterwards to watch the head being sewn on again. It was said of him that he was so obsessed by the ritual of hanging that it was his grisly habit in the dentist's chair to drop his handkerchief for the drawing of a tooth thus giving to his dentist the same sign of readiness that the condemned man gave to the hangman. "The most frightful particulars relating to suicide and murder; the investigation of the disfigured corpse; the sight of an acquaintance lying in his shroud seem to have afforded him a painful and unaccountable pleasure. When the first Lord Holland was on his death-bed, he was told that Selwyn, who had long lived on terms of the closest intimacy with him had called to inquire after his health. 'The next time Mr. Selwyn calls,' he said, 'show him up: if I am alive I shall be delighted to see him and if I am dead he will be glad to see me.' "

Although Selwyn was perhaps the most extreme of enthusiasts he was not alone in his taste for spectacles of death and cruelty—a taste which was in fact shared by many, if not most, of his contemporaries. They, perhaps, did not like to advertise their passion for these thrilling sights as widely as he did, but they enjoyed them none the less. Even those more serious men who did not think of the march to Tyburn as purely a matter for idle amusement believed that it was a sound and satisfactory institution. When it was abolished and executions became less a national sport, Dr. Johnson complained to Boswell, who was something of an *aficionado* himself, "Sir, executions are intended to draw spectators. If they do not draw spectators they do not answer their purpose. The old method was most satisfactory to all parties."

It was satisfactory perhaps for the condemned man, who found it easier to die bravely in the open, surrounded by a cheering crowd than to die alone and friendless, watched by a few officials, in the stark and dismal execution shed within the prison walls. Fielding described well the relationship between the criminal and his supporters. "The day appointed by law for the thief's shame," he wrote in his *Inquiry into the Late Increase of Robbers*, "is the day of glory in his own opinion. His procession to Tyburn and his last moments there are all triumphant; attended with the compassion of the weak and tender hearted, and with the applause, admiration and envy of all the bold and hardened. His behaviour in his present condition, not the crimes, how atrocious soever, which brought him to it, is the subject of contemplation. And if he hath sense enough to temper his boldness with any degree of decency, his death is spoken of by many with honour, by most with pity, and by all with approbation."

A few years later a Scottish clergyman described the same scene and came to the same conclusion. "Among the immense multitude of spectators," he wrote, "some at windows, some upon carts, thousands standing and jostling one another in the surrounding fields—my conviction is that, in a moral view, a great number were made worse, instead of better, by the awful spectacle. Of the ragamuffin class a large proportion were gratified by the sight; and within my hearing many expressed their admiration of the fortitude, as they termed the hardness and stupidity, of one of the sufferers. 'Well done, little coiner!' 'What a brave fellow he is!' "

When the body had been cut down the crowd would surge forward to touch it, believing that it had some peculiar medicinal qualities. Women would lift up the still jerking hand and brush it against their cheeks and a French visitor once noticed "a young woman, with an appearance of beauty, all pale and trembling, in the arms of the executioner, who submitted to have her bosom uncovered in the presence of thousands of spectators and the dead man's hand placed upon it."

After the hanging the hangman gave a party at an alehouse in Fleet Street when he sold the rope at sixpence an inch.

The hero's ovation which the condemned man was usually given and the brash and unrepentant behaviour expected of him are well described in Swift's *Clever Tom Clinch, Going to be Hanged*, 1727.

> As clever Tom Clinch, while the rabble was bawling,
> Rode stately through Holborn to die in his calling,
> He stopt at the George for a bottle of sack,
> And promised to pay for it when he came back.
> His waistcoat and stockings and breeches were white;
> His cap had a new cherry ribbon to tie't.
> The maids to the doors and the balconies ran,
> And said, "Lack-a-day, he's a proper young man!"
> But, as from the windows the ladies he spied,

Like a bow in the box, he bow'd low on each side!
And when his last speech the loud hawkers did cry
He swore from his cart "It was all a damn'd lie!"
The hangman for pardon fell down on his knee;
Tom gave him a kick in the guts for his fee:
Then said, I must speak to the people a little;
But I'll see you all damn'd before I will whittle!
My honest friend Wild (may he long hold his place)
He lengthen'd my life with a whole year of grace.
Take courage, dear comrades, and be not afraid.
Nor slip this occasion to follow your trade;
My conscience is clear, and my spirits are calm,
And thus I go off without prayer-book or psalm;
Then follow the practice of clever Tom Clinch
Who hung like a hero and never would flinch.

The spectators watched, not of course because it would improve their souls to watch, not because they might thus witness the true deserts of an evil life, but because they enjoyed it and it was the thing to do.

The spectacle of hanging was not then, nor ever had been, a deterrent. Human life was too cheap for that and the manner of death too heroic or too grotesque or too comic. For there was on occasion a distorted comedy about it all. The hangman, a condemned criminal pardoned for the express purpose of hanging, was as often as not drunk as he set about his task, and on one occasion had to be forcibly restrained from hanging the chaplain by mistake. For a good tip he would take more care, and as he was entitled to the clothes of the condemned man a well-dressed man received more respect than a beggar. As death was never instantaneous but came slowly through long suffocating minutes, friends of the condemned man would pull at his legs as he hung swinging from the gallows to shorten his agony. Sometimes the rope would break and the whole group would fall down to the ground in attitudes of gruesome absurdity.

The people who had come to watch Jack Sheppard suffer expected no scenes like these nor wanted them. As the young man stood there, his usually pale face quite white now in contrast with the blackness of his suit, the spectators were conscious of an unaccustomed sympathy, a strange pity. They watched as a man from Mr. Applebee's the printer's approached the cart and Jack handed to him the pamphlet which Mr. Defoe had written for him and which he had carried with him from Newgate. He said in a loud clear voice that this was his authentic confession and that he wished Mr. Applebee to print it for him. It was an effective advertisement. That night thousands of copies of the pamphlet were sold for a shilling each in the streets.

The end was close now. Beyond the ring of constables Jack saw the coach which Mr. Applebee had provided so that his young author should have a decent journey to the grave which waited for his body in St. Martin's churchyard. But Jack still hoped perhaps that the coach need not be used and that the surgeon who was going to try and bring back life to the body after it had been cut down would be successful in his task.

Mr. Wagstaff finished his prayers and giving his last blessing climbed down from the cart. The hangman tied the rope round one of the three cross-bars of the gallows and pulled the noose tight round Jack's neck. When the rope was in position he put a white handkerchief round Jack's forehead with a corner hanging down so that when Jack was ready to be "launched into eternity" he could pull the handkerchief over his face. The hangman jumped out of the cart and took up his position by the horse ready to lead it away as soon as Jack gave him the signal to do so. He looked at Jack standing still in the cart and waited for the signal, his hand on the reins by the horse's mouth. The noise and shouting died away to a murmur. The people stood still watching expectantly. The heads in Mother Proctor's Pews leaned forward. There was for a moment a strained anxiety, a nervous convulsive silence broken by a sudden incongruous laugh, a brief shout, a scream. For a moment only. Then Jack lifted his handcuffed hands to his face and pulled down the corner of the white handkerchief. The cart moved slowly away and Jack was left swinging helplessly, his legs jerking, his feet stretching frantically for a foothold in the unsupporting air.

He was so slight and the weight of his body exerted so little pressure on his neck, that it took several painful minutes for him to lose consciousness. "He died," a journalist reported with compassion the following morning, "with great difficulty and much pitied by the people."

He had been hanging there for a quarter of an hour when the spasmodic jerking of his body grew less violent and then ceased. As soon as the body fell still and relaxed a soldier leapt through the line of constables, who in sympathy made no effort to prevent him, and slashed through the rope with his sword. Taking the body in his arms he dashed away with it into the now frantic crowd. Several onlookers noticed that there were signs of life in the crumpled body.

The soldier, expecting opposition from the constables, quickly passed Jack to a friend farther back in the dense packed mass of people. And then the small unconscious body of Jack, his head hanging back from his shoulders, the red ugly rim round his neck plainly visible against the whiteness of his skin, could be seen being passed quickly from hand to hand over the heads of the crowd. A group of his friends standing towards the edge of the crowd waited impatiently for the body to be passed to them so that they could rush it to the surgeon. They shouted directions to the people who were handing the body back to them, but their intentions were misinterpreted. It was thought that they intended to take off the body to Surgeon's Hall for dissection, as was the usual fate of the corpse of a felon, and, hearing the dreaded word "Surgeon" shouted in furious voices above the din, the crowd became a frenzied mob.

Determined not to let the body of their hero fall into the devilish hands of the surgeons they fought for possession of it. Not knowing whom to trust it to or whom to snatch it from, the mob pulled it from hand to hand in a senseless frenzy of hysteria until it became obvious to his friends that they had "killed him with kindness" and were fighting over a corpse.

Meanwhile, believing that Mr. Applebee's hearse stood there to cart the body away for dissection, the people closest to it shouted curses at the driver. Tiring of shouting abuse they picked up stones and began to pelt him until he was forced to jump down for safety from his driver's seat and throw himself at them shouting his innocence. On all sides now the people turned towards the coach and attacked it with stones, and sticks and knives, breaking the doors and the spokes, smashing the sides in, ripping up the upholstery. The horses were released from the shafts and snorting and neighing in terror kicked up their legs and sent the screaming people flying in every direction. The coach was then pushed over on its side and its destruction completed.

A group of men, taking advantage of the diversion caused by the excitement round the coach, had by now managed to get possession of Jack's body and had carried it off. They marched with it, taking turns in carrying it, away from Tyburn and down the Oxford Road. Hundreds of people followed and the procession grew larger as they approached the town. The leading group carrying the

body turned off the Oxford Road into Bond Street and
marched along into Piccadilly. They turned left down
Piccadilly and across Leicester Fields into Long Acre,
where they entered a house under the sign of the Barley
Mow. Outside the house the hundreds of people who had
followed the body from Tyburn stopped and waited for
something to happen. Seeing them standing there rest-
lessly in Long Acre other people came up to join them
and to find out what they were doing there. Men and
women and children ran into the street from Leicester
Fields and Charing Cross and as the news spread from
farther afield. They poured out of the taverns and brothels
in Covent Garden and Drury Lane and from the rough
slums of St. Giles's and Whetstone Park. The murmur
grew to a roar.

It seemed to a few specialists in public disorder and
mob management that here was a good opportunity for
a riot. They spread a rumour about in the crowd that the
body of Jack Sheppard had been stolen and was being
hidden in a house in Long Acre until the commotion died
down and it could be taken out and sold to the surgeons.
The first bricks began to fly and the first shots to be
heard. Householders in Long Acre shuttered their windows and barricaded their doors as the shouts of the mob
became more menacing and as the noise increased. No
house was safe because few of the mob knew in which one
the body lay and soon it did not matter. They were not
interested in Jack Sheppard any more but in themselves.

They were obsessed now by the chance of loot, by the chance of finding something which they could safely steal in the uproar or by the opportunities of gratifying a lust for leadership or cruelty or excitement or destruction.

"A great many Justices met to concert proper Measures to preserve the Peace. The proclamation against Riots was read several times to disperse them, the Magistrates seeming loth to proceed to Extremities with the Giddy Rabble."

But the reading of the Riot Act had no effect upon the Giddy Rabble and an urgent message for troops had to be sent to the Savoy. Before the riot had got out of hand a company of footguards with drawn bayonets arrived at the top of Long Acre.

It was not yet dark and the troops moving down the street determinedly in the cold afternoon light soon brought the mob to its senses. The ringleaders were arrested. The rest slunk off back to their haunts to await their next opportunity. The crowds broke up and the people went slowly away. Another riot was over.

It was decided, however, not to risk any further outbreaks of violence and to delay the funeral of Jack until later on that night. Two soldiers were posted outside the door of the Barley Mow and were watched by a few sullen but quiet people. These onlookers saw just before dark an elm coffin being taken into the house where on a bed behind drawn curtains the body of Jack lay covered by a velvet pall.

At ten o'clock that night when the streets were quieter than usual a mourning coach drew up under the sign of the Barley Mow and the elm coffin was brought out of the house and placed inside the coach. A squad of foot-guards, as a precaution against further demonstrations, marched "with Bayonets fix'd at the Ends of their Muskets," on either side of the coach as it slowly rattled up the street. Before the coach had reached the junction of Long Acre and Leicester Fields, as if by instinct knowing what was happening, the crowd had collected again. But there were no demonstrations now. The people watched the slow-moving coach, the solemn mourners, the military cortège, as if they were paying their last respects to a great soldier. No one spoke. The iron rims of the wheels rattled over the cobbles making a strangely isolated noise in the unaccustomed quiet. A journalist noted the barking of a dog, the crying of a baby as distinct sounds, loud and sharp, emphasizing the silence.

The coach moved into the churchyard of St. Martin-in-the-Fields and the coffin was lowered into the earth.

The people who had watched the brief ceremony from behind the churchyard wall moved away and went back to their lodgings, to the brothels and gin cellars and doss-houses where the talk about Sheppard would go on all night and where all those who could afford it would soon be drunk on toasts to his memory.

Outside in the cold and narrow streets the ballad-mongers and the pamphlet sellers shouted their wares and urged the passers-by to read the true and wonderful story of their little hero. Tomorrow perhaps there would be another hero, so they made the most of the one they had that night. He was the greatest of them all, they said; a "Prometheus, something more than a man, a Supernatural."

BIBLIOGRAPHY

Account of Several Workhouses (1725).

ANDREWS, William. *Bygone Punishments* (1899).

ANGELO, H. C. W. *Reminiscences* (1828–1830).

An Answer to a Libel entitled A Discovery of the Conduct of Receivers and Thief-Takers in London (1718).

Authentic Memoirs of the Life and Surprising Adventures of John Sheppard (1724).

BESANT, Sir Walter. *London in the Eighteenth Century* (1902).

BLACKSTONE, Sir William. *Commentaries on the Laws of England* (1765–1769).

BLEACKLEY, Horace. *The Hangmen of England* (1929).

———— *Jack Sheppard*, with an epilogue on Jack Sheppard in literature and drama, a bibliography, a note on Jonathan Wild, and a memoir of Horace Bleackley by S. M. Ellis (Notable British Trials Series) (1933).

Bloody Register, The (1764).

BOSWELL, James. *The London Journal, 1762–1763* (1950).

British Gazette, The.

British Journal, The.

CAMPBELL, Lord. *The Lives of the Chief Justices of England* (1849).

A Candid Historical Account of the Hospital for Exposed and Deserted Young Children (1759).

CHANCELLOR, E. B. *The Eighteenth Century in London* (1920).

Daily Courant, The

Daily Journal, The.

Daily Post, The.

DEFOE, Daniel. *The History of the Remarkable Life of John Sheppard* (1724).

———*A Narrative of all the Robberies, Escapes, etc., of John Sheppard* (1724).

———*The True and Genuine Account of the Life and Actions of the Late Jonathan Wild* (1725).

DE SAUSSURE, César. *A Foreign View of England in the Reigns of George I and II.* Translated by Madame van Muyden (1902).

DE VEIL, Sir Thomas. *Observations on the Practice of a Justice of the Peace* (1747).

DICEY, W. *Life of Jonathan Wild, Thief-Taker General of Great Britain and Ireland* (1725).

Dictionary of National Biography.

DUDDEN, F. Homes. *Henry Fielding, His Life, Works and Times* (1952).

ENTICK, J. *A New and Accurate History and Survey of London* (1766).

FIELDING, Henry. *The Life of Mr. Jonathan Wild the Great* (1743).

———*An Enquiry into the Causes of the Late Increase of Robbers* (1751).

———*The Journal of a Voyage to Lisbon* (1755).

FIELDING, Sir John. *A Plan for Preventing Robberies within twenty miles of London* (1725).

FREEMAN, William. *The Incredible Defoe* (1950).

General Advertiser, The.

Gentleman's Magazine, The.

GEORGE, M. Dorothy. *London Life in the Eighteenth Century* (1925).

GORDON, Strathearn, and T. G. B. COCKS. *A People's Conscience* (1952).

GRIFFITHS, Arthur. *Chronicles of Newgate* (1884).

GROSLEY, P. J. *A Tour to London; or new Observations on England* (Translated from the French by T. Nugent, 1772).

HECHT, J. Jean. *The Domestic Servant Class in Eighteenth Century England* (1956).

The History of the Lives of Joanthan Wild, Thief-Taker, Joseph Blake, alias Blueskin, Footpad, and John Sheppard, House-breaker (1725).

HITCHEN, Charles. *The Regulator* (1718).

HOWARD, John. *The State of the Prisons in England and Wales* (1777).

IRELAND, John, and NICHOLS, John. *Hogarth's Works* (Edition of 1883).

JESSE, J. H. *George Selwyn and his Contemporaries* (1843–1844).

LECKY, W. E. H. *A History of England in the Eighteenth Century* (Edition of 1904).

LEE, William. *Daniel Defoe, His Life and Newly Discovered Writings* (1894).

LESLIE-MELVILLE, A. R. *The Life and Works of Sir John Fielding* (1935).

The Life and Adventure of Jack Sheppard, Executed at Tyburn (1724).

Lives of the Most Remarkable Criminals (1735).

London Chronicle.

London Daily Advertiser, The.

London Evening Post, The.

London Journal.

London Magazine.

London News.

Low Life, or One Half the World knows not how the Other Half Lives (1752).

Lyons, Frederick J. *Jonathan Wild, Prince of Robbers* (1936).

Magriel, Paul (Editor). *The Memoirs of the Life of Daniel Mendoza* (1951).

Malcolm, J. P. *Anecdotes of the Manners and Customs of London during the Eighteenth Century* (1808).

Mandeville, B. *An Enquiry into the Causes of the Frequent Executions at Tyburn* (1725).

Marshall, Dorothy. *The English Poor in the Eighteenth Century* (1926).

Morning Chronicle, The.

Newgate Calendar, The. (Various editions).

Old Bailey Sessions Papers.

Original Weekly Journal, The.

Parker's London News.

Phillips, Hugh. *The Thames About 1750* (1951).

Pringle, Patrick. *Hue and Cry* (1955).

Quennell, Peter. *Hogarth's Progress* (1955).

Radzinowicz, Leon. *A History of English Criminal Law* (1948).

Reith, Charles. *The Police Idea* (1938).

Richardson, A. E. *Georgian England* (1931).

Rouquet, Jean. *Lettres de Monsieur XX à un de ses amis à Paris pour lui expliquer les Estampes de Monsieur Hogarth* (1756).

St. James's Evening Post.

Schultz, W. E. *Gay's Beggar's Opera. Its Content, History and Influence* (1923).

Select Trials, 1720–1724 and 1724–1732.

Smith, Alexander. *Memoirs of the Life and Times of the Famous Jonathan Wild* (1726).

Snowden, W. Crawford. *London Two Hundred Years Ago* (1948).

Sutherland, James. *Defoe* (1937).

Sydney, W. C. *England and the English in the Eighteenth Century* (1892).

Trevelyan, G. M. *English Social History* (1944).

Turberville, A. S. *English Men and Manners of the Eighteenth Century* (1926).

Vilette, J. *The Annals of Newgate* (1776).

Walpole, Horace. *Letters* (Edited by Mrs. Paget Toynbee, 1903–1905).

Weekly Journal, The.

Welch, Saunders. *Observations on the Office of a Constable* (1754).

———*Proposal to render effectual a plan to remove the Nuisance of Common Prostitutes from the Streets of this Metropolis* (1758).

Wheatley, H. B. *Hogarth's London* (1909).

GLOSSARY OF CANT

autumn, n. A church or chapel.

babble, v. To make a confession or to inform against someone.

baggage man. A thief who carried away the loot after a robbery.

bank, n. A receiver.

battalions, n. Bands of pickpockets.

beaker, n. A silver tankard.

bit, n. A money bag or purse.

bite, v. or n. Cheat.

blow, v. See *babble*.

bone, v. To take.

bouser, n. A dog.

bowman, -en, a. Safe.

bulk, n. A decoy.

bundle, v. To tie a man up.

bunter, n. A prostitute.

buttock, n. See *bunter*.

buzz, n. A thief.

case, n. A house frequented by thieves, sometimes used to mean a brothel.

cast, a. Hanged.

catsing, n. A wig.

cheat, n. Rope.

chive, n. A knife.

chummage, n. Bribes and extortions levied by prison officials or fellow convicts upon a *rat*.

clank, n. A tankard.

clout, n. A handkerchief.

cole, n. Money, as in *queer cole*, counterfeit money, and *rum cole*, good money.

cove, n. A fool, usually a criminal's victim.

crop, n. See *cole*.

cull. See *cove*. Usually used in conjunction with another noun or adjective as in a *bridle cull*, a highwayman; a *queer cull*, a forger; a *quod cull*, a jailer; a *scout cull*, a watchman; a *nubbing cull*, a hangman.

dancers, n. Stairs.

darbies, n. Fetters or handcuffs.

diddle, n. Liquor.

dobe, n. A skeleton key.

dub, n. See *dobe*.

dudds, n. Linen.

fam, n. A ring.

famstring, n. A glove.

feeder, n. A spoon or fork.

file, n. A pickpocket.

finny, n. A funeral.

fisk, v. To search, sometimes *frisk*.

flat, n. A countryman, sometimes any simpleton.

foot-scamperer, n. A footpad.

gager, n. A rich man.

gammon, n. A *bulk* who took part in shop robberies.

garnish, n. See *chummage*.

glaze, n. A window.

glim, n. A candle.

glimmed, a. Burned in the hand.

gownman, n. A parson.

habbled, a. Arrested.

hoist, n. A shoplifter.

jacob, n. A ladder.

jagger, n. Gallows.

jigger, n. A door.

ken, n. A house; as in *boosing ken,* a tavern.

kid, n. A confidence trick.

lappy, a. Drunk.

lay, n. A profitable criminal activity; as in *filing lay,* picking pockets.

lift, n. A shoplifter.

lob, n. A box.

lock, n. See *bank.*

loge, n. A watch or clock.

lope, v. To climb.

lurries, n. Clothes.

make, v. To steal.

mause, n. A bundle.

mill, v. To rob.

mish, n. A shirt.

morris, v. and n. Dance.

Mount, the. London Bridge.

movables, n. Stolen goods.

munge, n. The dark.

nime, v. See *make.*

nubbed, a. See *cast.*

Old Nass. Bridewell.

pad, n. A bed.

peck, n. Food.

peepers, n. Eyes.

peery, a. Suspicious.

peter, n. A trunk.

pimp, n. A constable, sometimes a magistrate.

plumper, n. A professional perjurer.

poll, n. A wig.

pop, n. A pistol.

prancer, n. A highwayman.

prig, n. A member of the underworld.

push, n. A crowd.

rapp, v. To commit perjury.

rat, n. A newly arrested prisoner.

rattler, n. A cart or a coach.

reader, n. A book or pamphlet, usually a pocket-book.

ridge, n. Gold.

rum, a. Genuine.

run rusty, v. To betray.

scragged, a. See *cast*.

shap, n. A hat.

snabbled, a. See *habbled*.

sneaking-budge, n. A shoplifter.

snitch, v. See *babble*.

Spinning Ken, the. See *Old Nass*.

stamper, n. A shoe.

stock drawers, n. Stockings.

swag, n. A shop.

tail, n. A sword.

tatler, n. The moon.

tilt, n. See *dobe*.

toge, n. A coat.

toped, a. See *cast*.

truff, n. See *bit*.

tumbler, n. See *rattler*.

twang, n. A prostitute's bully.

wedge, a. and n. Silver.

whiddle, v. See *babble*, sometimes *whittle*.

Whit, the. Newgate. Named after Sir Richard Whittington, who left money for its rebuilding.

wipe, n. See *clout*.

INDEX

About the Author

CHRISTOPHER HIBBERT has made a particular study of the art and social history of the eighteenth century, which, he says, interests him more than anything else. His fascination with eighteenth-century backgrounds keeps him reading constantly; he is at present at work on another book on the London of the 1700's. He has had articles and short stories published in several periodicals and broadcast by the B.B.C.

Born in Leicestershire, England, in 1924, Mr. Hibbert was educated at Oxford University (Oriel College), where he took an Honours Degree in history. In World War II he became a member of the King's Royal Rifle Corps and was twice wounded during service as an officer with the Eighth Army in Italy, being awarded the Military Cross for his action against German fortifications on the Senio River. He is married, with three children, and lives near Henley-on-Thames.

This book was set in English Monotype Bell by

Clarke and Way, and printed by them

on Perkins and Squier Company's RRR Smooth Antique

made by P. H. Glatfelter Company.

The binding was done by The Haddon Craftsmen.

Typography and design are by Abe Lerner